ENCOUNTERING
DIVINE
PRESENCE

One Couple's Memoir of Pain, Death, and Joy

Beth H. Wilson, PhD & C. Brady Wilson, PhD

ISBN 979-8-88851-827-4 (Paperback)
ISBN 979-8-88851-828-1 (Digital)

Covenant Books
11661 Hwy 707
Murrells Inlet, SC 29576
www.covenantbooks.com

To those who have had cancer, to those who are living with cancer, and to their loved ones.

Also to those who have a "mystery illness," an illness that is not diagnosed by established medical lab procedures and/or diagnostics, yet suffer with chronic bodily pain, severe fatigue, chronic illnesses, and great uncertainty.

PREFACE

Generally, when tragedy comes, it is not only the person who suffers. Immediate family, friends, colleagues, extended family, and many others who are connected to the individual are highly affected. As you read about our illness journeys, you will see it was our immediate and extended families, friends, and colleagues who not only helped us but supported, comforted, prayed, and brought food when we thought we could not go on.

We have had very different illness journeys, as you will read in our stories. However, we have encountered divine presence, which for many people comes in various forms and ways, as it did for each of us. Whatever our and your paths are, an encounter with divine presence is always life-changing.

BRADY'S ILLNESS JOURNEY

Brady

Over the years, I have been guided, and my life has been enriched by the writings of those who have the gift of language. Among them are brilliant people whose words burned within me; authors like Ralph Waldo Emerson, C. S. Lewis, Owen Barfield, Saul Bellow, and Thomas Merton, as well as contemporaries like Richard Rohr and David Brisbin.

Recently, I came across this writing by Thomas Merton:

> [I]t was a lucky wind
> That blew away his halo with his cares,
> A lucky sea that drowned his reputation.
>
> Here you will find
> Neither a proverb nor a memorandum.
> There are no ways,
> No methods to admire
> Where poverty is no achievement.
> His God lives in his emptiness like an affliction.
> What choice remains?
> Well, to be ordinary is not a choice:
> It is the usual freedom
> Of men without their visions.[1]

---

[1] Thomas Merton, *A Thomas Merton Reader* (Image Books, Doubleday, 1989).

1

I hope that in reading the following experience from my life, you may understand what Merton's poem means to me, how it relates to my life and the life of my wife, Beth, and how I have sought to integrate it into my life and share it with our family and a few friends.

The Calm...

My wife, Beth, and I were living a great life in 2007. We had a nice home in Scottsdale, Arizona, and I had a vital full-time practice in clinical and forensic psychology in Scottsdale. Beth was working as a researcher in the healthcare industry, and the two of us were constantly involved in shared projects. Our son, Kristopher, and his family lived in Phoenix, and we saw them often. I used to spend hours playing with Ruby (our granddaughter) in our pool, and we shared many meals with our family on our patio. Our daughter, Kara, was in law school at the University of Arizona and was doing so well. She had a wonderful boyfriend, Tyler, of whom we thought the world. I have fabulous memories of holidays with family; Beth and I did what we could to support our kids.

The Hidden Threat

Little did I know in the fall of 2007 that my life would change forever in the next twelve months. For several years, my wife and I have traveled to central California to spend Thanksgiving with my parents. My parents were superb cooks, and even in their eighties would make the best, mouth-watering dressing, pies, and other scrumptious delights that we were eager to eat. It was a beautiful day in central California; the sky was a deep blue, and the leaves on the trees were turning bright red and yellow, adding to my magnanimous feeling of awe, beauty, and gratitude. After stuffing myself with the delectable, lovingly prepared meal, I lay down on the floor, of course, to watch the football game on TV.

When I lay down on the floor, I let my hands drop on my very full abdomen. It felt firm and a bit odd, but I didn't think much of it because I was so stuffed with luscious food. However, the firmness was only on the right side. Once we returned to our home in Arizona, I started pushing around on my abdomen; the firmness never went away. I told Beth about it, and I decided we should see a physician. So I called my family practice office to make an appointment with my doctor. He wasn't available, but I was able to see the nurse practitioner. She felt the firmness in my abdomen but was not sure what to make of it and suggested an ultrasound.

I suppose there were several reasons I was not really alarmed by the firmness I felt. First, I didn't have any symptoms that might lead me to think there was a reason for concern. Second, I was blessed with a really good health history, with few illnesses and a tendency to either fend off illness or recover very quickly if I became ill. My ongoing assumption was that this firmness was nothing to worry about and that whatever it was would soon and easily be resolved.

Beth and I went to a lab for the ultrasound. In preparation for the ultrasound, I was to drink a couple of glasses of water. After waiting for the fluid to find its way to my kidneys and then to my bladder, I was led into the room for the ultrasound. During the procedure, the ultrasound technician kept making "hmmm" sounds, which concerned me. *What*, I thought, *was she murmuring about?* During a break, she then asked that I drink more water, and indicated that she wanted me to drink enough so I would feel that I really "had to go."

During the ultrasound, the technician asked if I was having problems with my bladder—I was not. These questions were followed by more "hmmm" sounds from her. However, Beth and I left the office unconcerned. A few days later, I received a call from the nurse practitioner, whom I initially saw, informing me that she had received the ultrasound results. She said that there was a mass "in there" and that I needed to get a computed tomography (CT) scan. Still, Beth and I thought that perhaps I had a hernia. I continued to work, and we went on with our lives as if the "mass" was no big deal.

Let me say a word about denial. Denial can be a really good defense. All of us live in at least a small degree of denial that allows us to live with a certain amount of safety in what can be a treacherous world. I definitely had—and, to a certain degree, still have—the capacity for denial when faced with challenges in which I might otherwise wilt. I must be diligent to not enter into excessive denial yet preserve the defense so I can face life's challenges. This was the case during this episode in my life.

The CT scan was scheduled right away. We were thankful that our daughter, Kara, was with us at this time for winter break and accompanied us to the CT scan office. Our daughter knew that something was not right despite my and Beth's denial. I realize now I had a frivolous attitude about it all. I started making jokes about the iodine cocktail that I had to drink before the scan. After the CT scan was completed, the results were expected by Friday of that week. When that day came, we were all waiting for *the* phone call. I was at my office with Beth and Kara, who were sitting on the sofa. The call came from the nurse practitioner. Her concern was the size of the mass—it was *probably* cancer. It could be something else but was most likely cancer.

The three of us sat stunned in silence. It is interesting what happens in moments like this—moments of silence. All of us, with our thoughts racing in different directions, but experiencing the same consciousness, caught in a few moments of shared awareness of the grave entity that was cancer. I called my mother while Beth, Kara, and I were still in the office together. It was a powerful moment of strong emotion. I suspect the feelings I had were as strong as they were at least in part due to my awareness of my mother's own fragility and vulnerability this late in her life.

The three of us loaded up in the car and headed for home. Still in some denial, Beth and I were excited about Christmas and our family coming to Arizona to celebrate the holiday. Beth, Kara, and I went home that evening after receiving the "possible cancer" news and knew that we had better get busy making grocery and gift lists for the upcoming family Christmas; distraction is a wonderful coping tool. The three of us sat around the kitchen counter on the barstools, and I poured us all a glass of wine. Kara and I started writing the grocery list for myriad food and wine that we would need for Christmas Eve and Christmas Day and the days after. My wife and I were thrilled that Kristopher; our daughter-in-law; our precious four-year-old granddaughter, Ruby; and Kara would be with us for Christmas. Also adding to our Christmas joy was my wife's sister Shari, her husband, and two sons. Beth's sister and her family were coming in from the Midwest—a good time to be Arizona-bound. Our family is one of our deepest joys.

We prepared weeks in advance for the big day. I consider myself a good cook, having learned from my parents. My wife will attest that I am more practiced in the kitchen than she ever wanted to be. I spent time searching for perfect recipes and included some special dishes and shared recipes handed down from my mother and my wife's mother, who were lifelong friends even before Beth and I were born. According to the story handed down from both sets of parents, my wife's first laugh at about six months was at my parents' home, while I was on the floor playing with a bright new fire engine.

Beth got out the recipe box, which contained our mom's hand-written recipes on index cards. She went to the pantry and suddenly became very quiet. She then collapsed, heartbroken and crying, as the reality of it all hit hard. Kara and I went to hug her, and the three of us held each other for a long time before going back to our lists. My denial system was clearly more effective in defending me from the sinister possibility of cancer than were Beth's defenses. Beth is a sensitive and loving woman who feels things deeply. She was overwhelmed.

As Kara and I started writing our lists, Beth realized that the lists we were writing were organized in the exact same way and started laughing hysterically. Kara and I were organizing our lists according to where the grocery items were located in the store. We placed items on our lists in the order that we would find them as we walked through the store. Beth did not make her list this way and immediately determined that Kara and I were OCD about our grocery shopping. We all laughed so much that Beth's stomach ached. I had not laughed that hard and that much in a long time.

Kristopher

Our family had been looking forward to December for a long time. It was very exciting for us to be able to spend Christmas with extended family, whom we love so much. We always have fun and memorable experiences together. When we learned of Brady's diagnosis, it was sobering for all of us and put a pall over the celebration. At the same time, it almost didn't seem real. Was it possible that it could truly be as serious as it sounded? Surely not—Brady is tough, and he seemed to be in great health and spirits. Throughout the visit, I'm sure this was at the forefront of everyone's mind. But there was so much uncertainty, it was hard to process and reconcile the potential gravity of the situation with the joy we all felt in being together.

Kara

One of the truly divine decisions in my life was picking up and moving to Arizona for law school to be close to family, which then allowed me to be near Mom, Brady, and Kristopher during this time. The closeness and support of our extended family was felt deeply during that holiday. And the evening of epic and hilarious grocery planning before Christmas was a moment of comedic and cathartic relief that will stay with me forever. My role at the time of Brady's diagnosis was clear and continued throughout this story—remaining levelheaded and calm, bridging between Brady's fortitude and Mom's vulnerability.

Brady

We had a great Christmas with our family—paradoxically, as many moments in life are.

During our family's visit, I went through many tests. The nurse practitioner who had ordered the CT scan said I should see a surgeon immediately, which Beth and I did. Dr. Hashimoto was the surgeon who was recommended to us, but he was not an oncologist. He showed us the CT image of the very large mass in my lower right abdominal area and indicated that it was probably cancer. It was another likely confirmation, another blow, another reality hit.

During this time, our family was still with us during the days after Christmas. We all sat together one night and talked about what was happening. I felt so much support from everyone, which was a great comfort. Our discussion was supportive yet candid and matter-of-fact as to what might lie ahead. Our children are bright and well-educated. Beth and I knew that we were so rich in the personal resources of family and friends. At one point, I realized that, somehow, beyond my ability to understand it, I had been prepared for this moment. I told our family that I felt this and that I had no fear of it.

I have often reflected on this experience, and the fact that I had no fear of what was coming at this point, that I felt prepared. A number of things come to mind. I have long been aware that one thing that has prepared me to do the work with my clients, especially those who have experienced trauma, is my own readiness to move into their suffering and darkness with them. This "readiness" made it so much less difficult when anticipating what lay before me at this point. I found a clue to this when I came upon a poem by David Whyte called "The Well of Grief."

> Those who will not slip beneath
> the still surface on the well of grief,
> turning down through its black water
> to the place we cannot breathe,
> will never know the source from which we drink,
> the secret water, cold and clear,
> nor find in the darkness glimmering,
> the small round coins,
> thrown by those who wished for something else.[2]

During our visit with Dr. Hashimoto, he indicated that the surgery would most likely be highly complex and that the cancer should be treated with chemotherapy and radiation first. According

---

[2]   Used with permission from David Whyte (DavidWhyte.com).

to this doctor, it was imperative that the mass be shrunk prior to the surgery. We sought out a local oncologist for his opinion on how to proceed, assuming that some form of treatment like chemotherapy would be required before the surgery. The oncologist we consulted with gave us a completely different opinion. This oncologist said the mass needed to be removed immediately, with chemo and radiation after the surgery.

We were totally confused after having talked to these two reputable physicians. We still did not know what kind of cancer I had. A biopsy was ordered by Dr. Hashimoto and performed at a local hospital. At the hospital, at the same time, a CT scan was performed on my chest area. However, it did not even occur to me that there was the possibility of metastatic cancer, or that the cancer might be in my lungs. The CT scan for my chest was negative. I was relieved and alarmed simultaneously—alarmed at the possibility of metastatic cancer and relieved that the chest CT scan was negative.

The pathologists at the local hospital where the biopsy was performed were still uncertain of the kind of cancer I had. The biopsy was sent to a specialist at Emory University for analysis and a determination of the specific type of cancer. More waiting and wondering what I had. Where would we go? What were we going to do?

Shari

The first time I heard that Brady had significant health challenges was when I received a phone call from Beth, my sister, my only sibling. Beth spoke the dreaded words: "Brady may have cancer." As a nurse practitioner, I had heard this phrase many times spoken with a great uncertainty and fear for patients and families, and Beth's voice was no different. My family was busy preparing to leave for the Christmas holidays. We always looked forward to our Christmas holidays in Arizona with Beth and her family. How fun to get away from the dark and cold Indiana weather and fly into the sunny skies of Arizona. However, Beth's phone call changed everything. But once our family arrived on Christmas Eve to the Wilson home, we were surprised to find a celebratory mood, all the gorgeous

Christmas decorations, and the heavenly smells of the Wilson family gourmet holiday food preparations. There were extra warm hugs and smiles as we all greeted each other. The next day, I was able to spend a few moments with Brady.

Brady said he put his hands near his waist and hips, and he felt some kind of firm mass move from his back and into the pelvic area. He said it was a very odd sensation with no pain. His words were calm, measured, and informative. Beth came into the room and sat with us as Brady continued to share the information from the workup at that point. Brady allowed me to palpate the top of this mass, which was right of the periumbilical (around the navel) area. The mass was extremely firm, large, and smooth and was most likely cancer. After diagnosing breast and ovarian cancers, I unfortunately was very familiar with the dreaded feel of a cancerous mass.

After returning to Indiana, I was sitting in my office when Beth phoned with the final pathology report from the biopsy. It was sarcoma. My heart sank as the reality rolled over my mind and body. Sarcoma was a horrible diagnosis and almost always terminal. I needed to complete some more research but felt certain MD Anderson Cancer Center in Houston was Brady's closest and more promising referral. At the same time, I did not want to interfere with his doctors and Brady's supportive medical team. I was hoping the medical team would facilitate the referral to MD Anderson Cancer Center in Houston, Texas. It was a dilemma for me. I decided my role was to be supportive.

Beth and Brady began to talk about surgery first, then chemotherapy. As my concerns for Brady's life grew, I began to bring up the name of this amazing cancer institution in my conversations with my sister, Beth. I was hoping they would be open to at least investigating this option. Knowing my sister, I was sure she would begin her own research right away. I don't know how she brought it up with Brady, but I know that they were very conflicted in what their doctors were saying there. We talked about self-referral to MD Anderson Cancer Center in Houston. Upon his admittance to MD Anderson Cancer Center, I knew Brady was in a safe place—the best place—and that this institution would have the finest family-support systems in place for the incredible amount of stress our family would be experiencing.

Acceptance: First Step

Brady

In 2008, anyone could self-refer to MD Anderson Cancer Center in Houston, which I did. We had to send all the test results, documentation, and a tissue sample. We were very anxious to be accepted to the Cancer Center; we were confused, disoriented, not knowing where else to turn. I remember the day I received a call from the coordinator at MD Anderson Cancer Center asking if I could come. My response to her was "I'll be there tomorrow." It was a great relief—despite a very uncertain future. I ordered cookies for the coordinator and her staff to express our appreciation for their kindness and understanding.

Beth

During this traumatic time in our lives, I had been working at a well-known local health organization in Phoenix and conducting research on the future need for healthcare providers in the state. I loved my work and in fact had received a large salary increase in December 2007. I had health insurance through my employment for Brady and me, which made sense, since Brady was self-employed and his inclusion on my health insurance was less expensive. When I told my direct supervisor that my husband had a serious cancer, there wasn't much compassion or concern. I was told there was an "outlier" in the small organization, i.e., my husband's healthcare costs. The implication was that the agency would *not* cover my husband's health insurance.

As I sat in the office and heard these unbelievable words, thoughts of destitution and Brady's death ran through my entire shaking body. I asked for a break and went outside to call Brady. On the long elevator ride back up to the office, a gift came to me: the words "Tell them you will work on contract."

I rode the elevator up the thirty-some floors, went into the office, and sat down with senior members of the "team." I told them I would work on contract; they were elated and very glad to have me work on contract. Why the elation on the part of my supervisors? Contract work meant the company did not have to pay my healthcare insurance. The Consolidated Omnibus Budget Reconciliation Act of 1985 (COBRA) was our only option, which we did, and which costs a great deal of money. Brady and I spoke to a well-known attorney in Phoenix about this clear case of health discrimination; the attorney was stunned to hear our story of being shut out of the company's health insurance by this particular healthcare organization. We had clear evidence of health discrimination but did not pursue it, since Brady's life was most likely hanging in the balance. I did work on contract for a while until the stress of Brady's health was more than I could bear. I could not focus or complete the work that I needed to do. I had to quit the contract.

Kristopher

I remember feeling disbelief and shock at this situation with Mom's company and insurance. Unfortunately, I suspect that far too many cancer patients have had very similar experiences, which obviously creates unwelcome stress and undue hardship. It was very troubling to realize that access to the best care is anything but guaranteed, especially when the specifics of the diagnosis were so frightening. This was a very trying time for Brady and Mom, and there was a feeling of helplessness when I realized how much of this process might be out of their control in terms of getting the best care from the right people. Fortunately, they were led to the right place.

Brady

After what seemed like an eternity waiting for results from Emory University in Georgia, we were notified that the mass was a leiomyosarcoma—an aggressive and rare cancer. I immediately started researching what leiomyosarcoma was, and it was not good. I don't know how many times after reading about leiomyosarcoma, I thought to myself, *I wish I had not read that.* At the time of my diagnosis in 2008, there was a very high likelihood of death, and most people diagnosed with this type of cancer were dead in two years. In fact, the cancer was so deadly that it was considered a success if a victim survived two years. In the years since the diagnosis, I have heard of a few people who had been diagnosed with leiomyosarcoma, and they had all passed away.

Leiomyosarcoma is a soft-tissue cancer that grows from the muscle cells that line veins, arteries, bladder wall, bowel, uterus, stomach, and extremities; it can grow from any of these organs or sites. The mass was so large the physicians couldn't tell what the source was. Where was it growing from?

I have said for years that one of life's primary coping skills was the ability to live with ambiguity. The "not knowing" was wearing on me: first, the question of what this mass was; then what kind of cancer it might be; and now, what organ it had attached to. How could this be? I came to realize that I had coped with the news to this point by persuading myself that it was not cancer, that it would turn out to be a benign tumor. The cancer verdict was devastating enough, but the identification of this rare and aggressive cancer was information that extended me well beyond my coping ability.

The gravity of the diagnosis and the prospect of the cancer being fatal was something I was not prepared for emotionally, even with my system of denial intact. I could no longer minimize the potential severity of the diagnosis, nor could I assume safely that at some time in the future, everything would be okay.

I suppose that it is common for all of us to, at some time in our lives, confront our own mortality. Certainly, I know this from personal experience and the experiences of family and friends. Even more so, I have witnessed it in clients with whom I have worked over the last forty years. Yet the fact of being mortal (a cognitive experience) is somehow different from the experience of being compressed into a finite space of being fragile, vulnerable, and subject to nature's indifference or the perilous consequences of being a living being.

Just Do It

My maternal grandfather was a Scot. We called him Pop. Stoic in nature, Pop was sparing with his words. My mom was the same. She wouldn't say shit if she had a mouthful. I came about my stoic nature naturally. One of her favorite stories about me was about when I was not yet a year old and had colic. I wouldn't cry. Rather, I would stand in my crib and grunt.

When unable to cope, I would not shut down behaviorally. I suppose I would shut down emotionally. With the news of leiomyosarcoma, I went into "just do it" mode. I spent little time in reflection. I denied myself thoughts about the future other than the requirements of knowing that I had to "get things in order."

My only thought of the future was for Beth's well-being. I used to think about "making it" to almost seventy, and then dying before reaching seventy so that Beth would be okay financially. But I anticipated the worst. My grandfather (Pop), the Scot, died at sixty-one. My father-in-law (Beth's dad), died at sixty-two. I was sixty-one. Something told me there was some kind of destiny that was bringing me to a similar end.

A Foreign Land

Beth and I immediately made plane and hotel reservations, eager to get to Houston for help. Kristopher picked us up and drove us to the airport. There wasn't a lot of talking in the car or on the airplane that morning. It was our first time in Houston, and under these circumstances, great uncertainty produced great anxiety and concern over the unknown.

I recall the cab ride from the airport to the Cancer Center. Neither Beth nor I spoke. Never in my life had I felt so out of control and uncertain about the future. It was as if Beth and I were in a state of suspended animation, waiting for some sign to present us with the prospect of hope. This may have been the first time I fully understood the prospects and reality of having cancer. Finally approaching the numerous tall buildings and clinics at MD Anderson Cancer Center Houston's medical center drove the point home of the grave prospects of cancer.

The medical center was essentially a city in itself. There were blocks and blocks of large buildings, clinics, research centers, teaching, and administrative facilities that seemed to match the weight and size of what cancer meant to us—huge, foreboding, ominous, unknown, looming.

Though silent, I knew that both Beth and I were struck at this time by the enormity of the diagnosis. Even now as I read over my story, I am reluctant to type out the word *cancer*. Though I have accepted the diagnosis, I resist memorializing it. The scene of the medical center in Houston, containing MD Anderson Cancer Center, imposed upon both me and Beth an understanding of what enormous resources would be required to address this alien thing growing inside me. We sat silently in the taxi, the medical center looming in front of us and drawing closer. With each mile, we felt ourselves advancing on something unknown that would dictate for us the circumstances of our lives for months and years to come.

I didn't want to reveal my sense of unease to Beth because I knew that she was, to some degree, reliant on my "being strong," or at least appearing to have adequate control of myself in order to navigate the uncertainty before us. This was a vastly different feeling than I had ever felt before. I had gone through difficult and uncertain times before, but they never represented an existential threat. This was existential. Suddenly, even brutally, the reality was right in front of me that I might die, that Beth might be left alone, that our family would be abandoned, that our friends would be left, that my clients and work partners would have lost someone who had provided them with some help. I realized that I was not worried for myself, but I was for Beth and the kids. I did not want to think about what my death might mean to Beth in particular.

Beth

Driving up to the clinic/hospital area, I saw people from all over the world, many dressed in their country's cultural mode of dress. I was amazed at the size of the area and astounded at the number of people seeking help. I was scared, overwhelmed, had a great deal of anxiety, and wondered why so many people had cancer. Why does Brady have such a rare cancer? My legs were weak. Would the doctors here be able to help, and would they know about leiomyosarcoma? Would he live? I was nauseated.

Brady

Looming, I suppose, is an operative word. Beth and I did not know what was before us. Looming in our future was the cancer treatment about which we were uncertain. Looming before us was whatever consequences there would be from treatment or the cancer itself. Looming before us were changes or losses that we *felt* coming but could not predict. Not knowing what might be in our future, we were prevented from doing much in preparation or in response. Hopeful, dreading, we entered what seemed like a version of Oz—a foreign land with an unknown language and unfamiliar people who held my life and our future in their hands. We felt helpless in a way, and the days to come would slowly draw from our grasp our ability to control our lives and take us to the point of release and submission.

The first day was comprised of tests—lab tests, positron-emission tomography (PET) scans, and a chest X-ray. The initial lab tests were designed to screen for certain "markers" that might indicate cancer. Also, they would provide my physicians with basic information as to how fit a patient I was upon entering treatment.

The PET scan is designed specifically to look for cancer. It is an interesting test. Cancer loves sugar. So radioactive isotopes are bound to sugar molecules, and the sugary liquid is injected into the veins. The cancer "gobbles" up the sugary molecules, and under the scan, the cancer lights up like a Christmas tree. The chest X-ray is meant primarily to look for any evidence of metastatic cancer that might reside in the lungs.

The next morning, Beth and I went to meet with the MD Anderson Cancer Center oncologist for the first time. We didn't know the process, but the physician specialists made decisions as a group. The oncologist, the radiologist, the surgeon, physician assistant (PA), and other staff met as a team to look at the test results and decide about treatment. Prior to meeting with the oncologist, we went in and met with the PA. The PA was very blunt. The cancer was very serious, and I might be a candidate for a "cure." A cure meant possibly two more years of life. Her next words sent chills and shudders down our bodies: "We are going to treat you as an inpatient and bring you close to death. Your white cell count will go to zero, and you will be here for several months."

There were two more tests to do that day, and we would not meet with the oncologist until the next day. We went back to the hotel and could not speak; we were in shock.

Beth

We will bring you close to death.

Hearing these words from the PA was mind-numbing. I felt like this entire situation was not real. I wanted to scream at her, but I could not speak. I just sat there, feeling very nauseated. Back at the hotel, neither Brady nor I spoke. I didn't have a voice. My mind was racing: what if Brady didn't make it. "Bring him close to death"? Were they serious? Why did they have to do that? I could not ask questions; I was literally speechless. We would have to sell the house. What if we couldn't? How were we going to pay the bills? The scary thoughts kept racing; I could not stop them.

Brady

What do you say to the person you love more than anything else in the world at a time like this? How much of your own pain are you willing to share or impose on them? Beth and I have spoken of this afterward, but given that we were each overwhelmed, we dared not speak of it lest we destroy one another, or, by the utterance, devastate ourselves by "making real" the thing by saying it out loud.

Exhale

The next day, we returned to MD Anderson Cancer Center, and a different PA came into the office this time. The plan had changed; he told us that I could get chemotherapy back in Phoenix. Our new oncologist at MD Anderson Cancer Center, Dr. Deka Araujo, would provide the exact chemotherapy to be administered and manage the process from Houston. Our oncologist, Dr. Araujo, would track the progress of chemotherapy, and then I would go back to Houston for radiation, endure a waiting period, and then surgery to remove the leiomyosarcoma. Wonderful news! We could go home for now. We finally met with Dr. Araujo, an excellent physician and wonderful person, whom we grew to deeply admire and respect.

Dr. Araujo would become such a big part of our lives. When we first met Dr. Araujo, Beth and I related to her our journey to that point. We spoke of the differing opinions we had received. We spoke of the fact that we could not find an oncologist or surgeon who knew much at all about leiomyosarcoma. Dr. Araujo sensed our uncertainty, bewilderment, and apprehension. Kindly, she interrupted us. She said, "So that you know, I have six other cases of leiomyosarcoma on the floor today."

At last! We were in the right place. Dr. Araujo understood. We were in the midst of an enormous resource, and we felt embraced and hopeful. All around us now was knowledge and expertise rather than uncertainty. All around us were affirming messages and direction rather than the shrugs of physicians who might have been well-meaning but not knowledgeable.

During our visit, we also met with Dr. Raphael Pollock, a phenomenal surgeon, who told us my surgery was what the surgeons called "MOAS"—the mother of all surgeries—scary yet funny. Dr. Pollock told us that if the surgical team were able to get the appropriate margins that there was an eighty percent chance of a cure. Beth and I were ecstatic! For the first time, we had hope!

He gave me his phone number. He had just spent an hour talking with us. He encouraged us to call whenever we had questions or concerns. We never called, but the fact we knew we could meant so much.

I am very fortunate to have relationships with several physicians in Phoenix, so once we returned home, we received several leads. I contacted doctors whom I knew to receive a referral for an oncologist to manage the chemotherapy. I called the surgeon we had met earlier in the process, Dr. Hashimoto, to do a minor surgery to place a catheter in the upper left part of my chest under the skin. The chemo would be inserted via the port and enter the blood system quickly. Within a week, the port was inserted, and chemo began. I didn't know how much time I could devote to my practice, and I did not know what effects the chemo would have on me; there were many unknowns. But we continued.

Beth

After Brady's initial visit with Dr. Deka Araujo at MD Anderson Cancer Center in Houston, he was able to receive chemotherapy in Phoenix. Our first visit to the Virginia Piper Cancer Treatment Center in Scottsdale, we were excited, and I met with the insurance office, while Brady met with the chemotherapy nurse. However, I was told that our insurance would not cover Brady's chemo. The COBRA plan was with a nationally recognized insurance company. We had felt very confident with this nationally known health insurance plan; but not paying for Brady's chemo assured his death.

The chemo would have cost between $5,000 and $10,000 *per chemo session*. My knees were weak, my heart raced, and I waited for Brady to take a break with the chemotherapy nurse. While I was shaking and nauseous, I told him COBRA wouldn't pay for his chemo. Then I went back into the insurance office at the Scottsdale Cancer Treatment Center. In explaining to the insurance office that Brady's order came from the Sarcoma Center at MD Anderson Cancer Center in Houston, I asked that the insurance office call them. After that call to the Sarcoma Center at MD Anderson Cancer Center in Houston, the health insurance company deferred to MD Anderson Cancer Center in Houston. COBRA would pay for Brady's chemotherapy.

I cannot explain the physical, emotional, and mental release that we had after this news—as anyone would in the same or similar situation. However, there are many people whose health insurance will not cover care for life-threatening diseases and illnesses. The *only* reason Brady's claim for chemotherapy would be covered was because of the acknowledged expertise at MD Anderson Cancer Center in Houston. If the health insurance company would not have covered his chemotherapy, we would have had two choices: let him die or go deeply into debt and, ultimately, bankruptcy. We were fortunate; most people aren't as fortunate.

Brady

It was challenging to tell my clients about my cancer, but they needed to know and make other arrangements if they chose. I knew I would begin to look ill. A couple of clients decided to see someone else, but most of my clients opted to hang in there with me as I went through the chemo, hair loss, and lifestyle changes. I continued to work full-time, play golf, and exercise during the chemo process.

One day, I got up (which was hard to do many mornings), got in the shower, started washing my hair, and looked down. My hair was all over the shower floor—and everywhere else where I had walked. I thought, *So this is how it happens.* I went to the barber and just had him buzz off the rest. I would rather be bald than have the stringy look. Not long after our five-year-old granddaughter saw me bald, she said to Beth, who was beside her, "Grandma, Grandpa looks really different." And I did!

The next few months consisted of chemotherapy treatment and making lifestyle changes. I worked at my practice during the chemo process with no hair but also no nausea. I was very grateful for the lack of nausea, which, of course, made my work possible. I did begin to look a little green, however.

I don't know why, but it really did not bother me to lose my hair, or even to begin to look a little green. I suppose it was, at least in part, because those around me, especially my family, didn't look at me with a look of horror or surprise. I was not self-conscious, but I must admit that I thought baldness was easier for me as a male since baldness was so often a choice by men at the time.

Beth

The pain in my chest was profound when Brady began to look a bit green and his hair fell out, but I wanted to be cheerful for Brady's sake and told him over and over that he looked fine. He really did look fine without hair. But the change in skin color reminded me all too well of the villain inside the love of my life and my soulmate. My heart broke every time I looked at him, but the smile on my face tried to bridge the ache. It was very hard to smile.

Brady

We put our house up for sale in 2008 and repeatedly reduced the price as the recession loomed over the country—another grim reality. We just could not sell the house, but we were blessed to have a wonderful realtor, Carol, who not only took good care of our house but took care of our sweet dogs when needed and became a wonderful friend. We are grateful to her. Her care of our rescue dog, Zoe, and our golden retriever, Chip, was so very helpful. Carol was a gift.

Beth didn't know it, but whenever we looked at a place we might buy and move into during treatment and live in afterward, my private criteria for deciding was whether it would be a good place to die. I would always go to the master bedroom, look for the best window, and determine if there was something I could look at if bedridden. I wanted to be able to see out to something living and/or beautiful.

Was It Working?

After six weeks, it was time to go back to MD Anderson Cancer Center to determine the effectiveness of the chemotherapy treatment and have a PET scan to check the state of the tumor. Beth and I were quite anxious about the trip. During this time, we had family, friends, and an army of people praying for me—people we knew and those we didn't. We floated on those prayers for a long time. Dr. Araujo said that she needed to see the comparison of the PET scan (before and after the chemo treatment) and that she needed to see evidence that the chemo was affecting the tumor and/or starting to kill the cancer.

I remember waiting in the exam room to see Dr. Araujo. Beth and I were both anxious about the results of the chemo. I know that we were both scrutinizing the expression on her face when she entered. Did she look serious (a sign of bad news)? Was she smiling (good news)? Her words will never be forgotten: "It's working, it's working!"

Tears of joy ran down Beth's face.

Beth

My stomach was in knots waiting for Dr. Araujo to come into the room. Never had I been so afraid and hopeful at the same time—such a strange feeling. I was shaking, I was so nervous. Then to hear "It's working!" was almost unreal.

We had been through so much at that point, I couldn't believe it, but it was real, and all I could do was cry. Cleansing, releasing tears. The knots in my stomach and the shaking in my body started to dissipate.

Brady

We went back to the Rotary House where we were staying, which is a hotel connected by a skybridge to the Cancer Center. The Rotary House is a wonderful place for patients and family. We celebrated: Beth had a glass of wine, and I had a beer, which I had not had in quite some time.

At this point in time, we were very grateful, but I was worried about my practice. I was not able to bring in as much money, and the trips to Houston were costly, as were stays at the Rotary House. I was about three months into chemo, and one day, I had lunch with a wonderful friend who had been through severe health problems. He gave me a book at lunch, and later I discovered a check hidden in the pages. The gift would support and help with our living expenses for several months. I cannot overstate what this meant to me and to Beth. We are eternally grateful to our friend who helped us in our time of need. Money was raised from loving family and friends to help us and was gratefully and graciously received.

One of the things I continued to enjoy was gardening. I loved gardening and worked hard to beautify the backyard, which was lush with flowers, two big trees, green grass, and bougainvillea. Working in the yard typically energized me. But one Friday, as we were relaxing on the back porch, I became extremely fatigued. I was beginning to feel what I thought were the effects of chemo. To this point, I had held up pretty well while going through the transfusions. When I began to feel weak, I didn't know what else to attribute it to other than the chemo.

The next morning, I did not have the strength to get out of bed. The fatigue was terrible. We called Dr. Araujo; she said it could be an embolism and that we should get to the hospital. We went to the emergency room (ER) at a hospital close to us, and I was checked in. The ER physicians were not sure what was happening. Beth sat and watched as my blood pressure continued to decrease. It was a hospitalist who correctly diagnosed my condition—pulmonary toxicity.

My breathing capacity was extremely low. The imaging of my lungs revealed what was called a ground-glass shadow, indicating pulmonary dysfunction. I was not getting oxygen. The toxicity was from the chemotherapy. I was only halfway through the course of the chemo, but my oncologist said that I needed to discontinue the chemo, which I did. I was able to leave the hospital after a few days and began to gain a little more strength. But now what? I had to discontinue chemo? My options were becoming more and more limited.

During the growing season of 2008, something quite odd was happening to the flowers and greenery in the backyard. At about the same time that I was starting radiation treatment, many of the plants did not bloom and were wilting. This had never happened before in the eight years we had lived in the house. Most of the leaves were turning yellow; many of the plants looked anemic. I could not figure out what was going on. I tried experimenting with different watering schedules and feedings. I took leaves into the plant stores and asked professionals what they thought was going on; they didn't know.

The wilted plants were very noticeable all that spring and into the summer. No one had an explanation, but in my mind, the plants rather looked the way I felt.

Kristopher

This was such a difficult time for all of us who knew and loved Brady—even though we were all aware of his diagnosis and the hard road he had to travel, this was the first time he really seemed physically weak and vulnerable. In particular, it was disheartening to know that even though the chemo was working, he couldn't continue with it.

I remember visiting him in the hospital when he was recovering from the pulmonary toxicity and being so saddened by his weakened condition—he was most certainly not himself physically. However, Brady never failed to smile or ask us how we were. He lifted our spirits in a way when we came to see him, even through all the pain he must have been experiencing. This was very inspiring, and I'll never forget his inner strength and positive attitude throughout this ordeal.

Golf and Radiology

Brady

We returned to MD Anderson Cancer Center to see Dr. Gunther Zuntag, the radiologist, in May of 2008. I needed to start daily radiation treatment in Houston for six weeks, with Saturdays and Sundays off. I lived in a hotel about a mile and a half from the clinic, so I would walk daily to radiation treatment. There was a golf course on the other side of the clinic, and I would go over and hit golf balls for about a half hour and then walk back to the hotel. I was walking two to four miles a day and decided I would try to get myself as fit as I could and prepare myself for surgery. I was feeling optimistic; even though significant negative effects can result from the pulmonary toxicity, such as emphysema or chronic obstructive pulmonary disease (COPD), I had none of these. I was very fortunate that in a few weeks, the toxicity had cleared up. I felt stronger and better not having chemo and being able to exercise. And the chemo had been successful!

I would go to the clinic at the hospital in the mornings and find a spot near the MD Anderson Cancer Center coffee center, order a yogurt and coffee, get on Wi-Fi, and piddle around to keep my mind busy. I talked with other cancer patients until it was time for radiation and then walk back to the hotel room and fix myself a meal.

Talking with other cancer patients was incredible. These were some of the most optimistic, positive, grateful people I have ever met. It was wonderful group therapy! They were all going through different types of cancer, and I met with some of their families. It was such a positive experience; having the other patients and the doctors in the same place, I felt a real sense of community and safety.

In the months and years after the surgery, I have returned to MD Anderson Cancer Center in Houston for checkups. Beth has asked me if going back is traumatic for me, and it never is. MD Anderson Cancer Center is my safe place. I was so well taken care of there. The diagnosis was understood, the treatment was embraced, and I felt safe.

As I was walking back from radiation to the room one day, I had an epiphany. There is an immediate dissonance in your mind when diagnosed with cancer because the medical team wants the patient to accept that you have cancer. The doctors say that, otherwise, many people put off treatment or don't attend to themselves, so there is a real effort by the medical team to encourage you to embrace the diagnosis. But the whole point of the diagnosis is to get rid of the cancer. It is a bit strange to radically accept the diagnosis so that you can effectively fight the cancer. I talked with one of my surgeons about this paradox, and he understood.

My radiation lasted six weeks. I had been told that there were side effects from the radiation that could be unpleasant. However, during this time, I was recovering from the side effects of chemotherapy, so I was doing better rather than worse. Near the end of the course of radiation, I did notice it was like a sunburn on my posterior side, opposite the tumor. I later experienced the effects of the radiation on the nerves that extend into the groin and pelvic region. I had a kind of confusion about the feedback I was given by my body regarding bladder, bowel, and sexual functions. I would detect that something was happening but was unable to discriminate among the functional demands. I didn't know if I had to urinate, if I had to defecate, or if I was aroused. All I knew was that I needed to get to a bathroom, and then I would know. The nerve bundle from the sacral spine that controls bladder, bowel, and sexual functions had been affected by the radiation. I became concerned that there might be long-term damage.

Beth

During Brady's time away, I felt that I was being prepared to live alone. I did not tell Brady about this feeling. I was working at a different organization during this time, which helped to keep my mind somewhat off what Brady was going through in Houston, but only somewhat. The deep, relentless, soul-breaking fear that ran through my body and mind is hard to describe. We had re-met in 1998 after having had a moment on the beach in Michigan when we were young; we were married in 2000, and for seven glorious years we had a wonderful life, and now this! Rage at God, fear of losing Brady…my heart was breaking. It was hard to sleep; my mind spiraled out of control anticipating the worst and praying for the best.

Brady

I never disclosed to Beth that I believed I needed to prepare for my death as well.

Cooling Off for Surgery

There was a "cooling off" period following radiation prior to surgery. I never learned what this meant. I didn't know if time was required for tissue to recover before surgery and after radiation, or if I was radioactive. During this time, Beth and I went back to Houston to meet with all five of the surgeons on my team who would be part of my surgery: Dr. Raphael Pollack, the chief surgeon; Dr. Garrett Walsh, a thoracic surgeon; Dr. H. Barton Grossman, a gastrourinary surgeon; Dr. Egbert Pravinkumar, an anesthesiologist; and Dr. Lawrence Rhines, a neurosurgeon. There was also a physical exam performed by an internist, Dr. Shuwei Gao, to make certain that I was healthy enough to survive a major surgery. When I met with Dr. Pollack, he indicated to me that he and the team did not know what the blood source was for the tumor. In other words, the cancer had to be growing from something, but the surgeons didn't know from where it was growing and would not know until the surgery. Hence, a neurosurgeon was on hand in case it was growing from the sacral spine, and a gastrourinary surgeon was needed because of the proximity of the tumor to the bladder.

He also told me there would be a wound nurse available at the meeting. The wound nurse told us about what to expect if removal of the colon and/or bladder was necessary. The surgical team would have to "tattoo" me on my abdomen because there was the prospect that when I came out of surgery, I might not have a bladder or a colon. If so, there would be two stomas, or openings, where two bags would be placed: one for the bladder and one for the colon. Beth was with me when we discussed this possibility with Dr. Pollack and was quite distressed. I was not as distressed; I was trying to make the best out of the situation and made a joke about not having to use as much toilet paper—a bad joke, and probably trying to engage in some denial.

We were scheduled to meet with the anesthesiologist. There were certain tests that I had to do, such as leaning my head back to make sure that my airways were open so there would be no problem being intubated during surgery. While we were meeting with the anesthesiologist PA prior to meeting the anesthesiologist, she hesitated at the door, looked at us, and said, "By the way, how did you get the chief?" Beth and I were bewildered and must have looked it. We wondered if it was a nickname or something. The PA must have noticed our bewilderment and told us that Dr. Pollack was the Chief of Surgical Oncology. We realized that we were incredibly fortunate to have Dr. Pollack as our chief surgeon, but also, each member of our surgical team was an expert at MD Anderson Cancer Center in their medical specialty. We were amazed and bewildered that we had these kinds of resources.

The Mother of All Surgeries

The day before surgery, our son and daughter, Kristopher and Kara, and Beth's sister, Shari, came to be with us. We were very thankful that they came; we could not have made it through the surgery without them. We had two rooms at the Rotary House: one for Beth and me, and the other for the family. The evening before surgery, I had Jell-O, chicken broth, and a fabulous (!) bowel-cleansing liquid, while the rest of the family was playing a board game and laughing hysterically. Such a paradox... So much anxiety yet laughter for Beth and the family was really good—emotional release! Though I couldn't be a part of it (due to bowel cleansing!), I could hear them, and it helped me cope.

At 5:30 AM on Tuesday, we headed over to surgery, where we waited with many other families with different kinds of cancer. I had chosen a hat given to me by Kara and Tyler that had a lot of "cancer-beating juju" assigned to it. Some families were there with spouses, some with children, some with parents. No one was talking. Everyone was very sober; the somberness in the room was palpable. Finally, I was called in and gave hugs and kisses to our children. Beth was allowed to come with me, and surgery preparation began.

Devices were put on my legs to keep the muscles moving, so I would not "throw a clot during surgery." The anesthesiologist came in and told me that in addition to anesthesia, they would be giving me an epidural because this surgery was so disruptive to the entire abdominal cavity. Everything from my ribs down would be removed and set aside and placed on a surgery table while our surgeon performed the delicate dissection. They would have to cut through a great deal of tissue, so there would be a lot of pain afterward. The chaplain came by and said a prayer with us, and then it was time for me to go and for Beth to leave after hugs and kisses. They had started a drip on me, so I was beginning to feel a little groggy, but they had to keep me conscious until the epidural was placed. An epidural is an injection of medication into the spinal area. In my case, the medication was a numbing agent.

I was then wheeled into the operating room. It was smaller than I thought it would be. It had windows at the top, so I assumed that was for surgical fellows to observe the procedure. The amazing thing was that there were stacks and stacks and stacks of tools—surgical equipment—which was surprising but also reassuring. It was incredibly bright, so much so that even though sedated, I had to squint my eyes. I began looking around the room for my surgeon and his team but could not recognize anybody thanks to the masks, goggles, and other protective gear.

They moved me off the gurney, and I was placed on the surgical table. It was interesting; the table was very narrow and reminded me of a cross. My arms were placed at a ninety-degree angle from my body. I was lying there motionless, waiting for whatever was next in the procedure. I was not anxious. This was the day we had been waiting for over eight months. The tumor would finally be removed, and we would have a better idea about our future.

Before losing consciousness, the epidural was given so that upon awakening, I would not experience the pain from the surgical insults to my body. An incision would open me up from the sternum to the pubic bone—as far north and south as one can get. Then I would be opened up left and right so that the surgeons had good and open access to my abdomen and pelvis. This meant that there would be a massive physical assault on my abdominal and pelvic regions. Hence, the epidural.

After the epidural, I was asked to start counting backward from ten. The anesthesiologist was very soft-spoken, as if not wanting to arouse me in any way.

A note here: The night before the surgery, I did not sleep much. I can't say that I was anxious, just excited. Beth and I had come so far to get to this point, and we both understood very well that my prognosis and our hopes weighed heavily on the outcome of the surgery. Then, the night before the surgery, I was up all night doing the bowel cleanse. I didn't get a wink of sleep. As I was lying there in the operating room, surrounded by surgeons, nurses, and exotic-looking tools, I wasn't anxious. I was just very eager to get to sleep. I started counting out loud from ten, nine…and then I do not remember anything until I was in recovery.

I woke up in recovery alone. No one was there with me at the time. I heard voices, but I believe I was there with others who had undergone surgery, along with their surgical teams. I wanted to go back to sleep, but I was too curious about the surgical outcome to do so.

Someone from the medical team came out every hour or so to report to the family how things were progressing. Either a nurse or one of the surgeons would appear and talk to my family. This was a wonderful comfort and support for them.

Beth

Brady's surgery was so long—sixteen hours. Every hour seemed to drag like ten hours. Each time a nurse or one of the surgeons came out, my heart would skip a beat; knowing that this was the "Mother of All Surgeries" was extremely scary. However, each time one of the medical team came out, they provided a good report, indicating Brady was tolerating the surgery well. Tears and "Thank God," was my response. Then back on edge until the next medical team visit.

When one of the surgeons came out, it looked like he (all were male) had been in a war. I had met each surgeon in the hospital (i.e., not while performing surgery), and clearly each one was working so hard; it showed on their faces, in their sweat, and in their eyes. I was almost speechless as I saw each surgeon, and I was very thankful for each one of them.

Dr. Grossman, the gastrourinary surgeon, had quite a bit of work to do. The mass, which was five pounds, the size of a grapefruit, was growing from Brady's ureter, the tube connecting the right kidney to the bladder. It was a growing tumor, so it was just pushing other organs aside. Brady was asymptomatic for years while this tumor was growing. Part of the ureter had to be removed, and the remainder of the ureter had to be stretched and reattached. A stent had to be inserted from the kidney to the bladder to hold it all together. Since the chemotherapy and the radiation had begun to kill the tumor, the tumor had formed a kind of "rind" around itself. It was essentially encapsulated. This was helpful; there were no active cells that could be disrupted during the surgery.

Kristopher, Kara, Shari, and I would all take turns going to get food from another floor in the hospital and bring it back so we wouldn't miss the team visit. There were TVs, lounge chairs, couches, and chairs; we would walk around the waiting area, which was quite large. Many families were waiting. However, as we waited, we saw all of them leave, since most didn't have sixteen-hour surgeries. More angst and pain in my stomach. I called Brady's parents and my mom to give a progress report, since they were not able to be there. As usual, they were very thankful and kept praying.

Kristopher

MD Anderson Cancer Center in Houston is a remarkable place. It was amazing to see such a large community of cancer patients, families, and caregivers with a common goal of comfort and healing. Although it was obvious that all the patients there were in varying degrees of pain, physical and emotional, there seemed to be a shared spirit and energy of hope and purpose. The doctors, nurses, and staff all seemed like extraordinary people and provided excellent care, none more so than Brady's surgeons, doctors, and nurses. It was great to meet them and thank them.

The day of waiting during the surgery was difficult—it was long and nerve-wracking—but it was good that we were all together. I think we all believed that there was a very good chance of an excellent outcome, but anything could happen. We were confident in those who were caring for Brady, and in his capacity to get through the surgery. As I mentioned, he is tough.

Kara

After hearing so much about MD Anderson Cancer Center and Brady's and Mom's experiences there, and having anticipated the surgery for quite a while, I felt an odd mix of excitement along with significant anxiety as I flew into Houston and made my way to meet them. No matter how challenging the reason, there is always joy in bringing us together. The long day of waiting while Brady was in surgery was intense for all of us, but we especially tried to keep Mom's spirits up. We appreciated the regular updates from the staff and finally hearing from the surgeon after they were finished. We understood it would be a challenging recovery, but the surgery had been as successful as we could have hoped.

Shari

I flew into Houston and met Kara, my niece, and Kristopher, my nephew, to be with Brady before the surgery and Beth during it. I did not know until the day of surgery that Brady would have at least five surgeons involved in his case. As wonderful as the state-of-the-art images (i.e., PET, MRI, CT scans) are, there is nothing like seeing a mass in real time after dissection into the skin and muscle. The ugliness of a large tumor is humbling to the surgeon. The possibility of cystectomy (bladder removal), partial colon resection, possible vascular resection, etc., were all part of planning for the sixteen-hour surgery.

The waiting room looked a scene of extremely organized chaos. The volunteers attending to the families were kind and compassionate, but busy. The extremely large room was full of light and warmth. One area was filled with computers to communicate with extended family, friends, ministers, and communities waiting to "hear the news." As the hours and minutes on the clock marched ever so slowly forward, we noticed we were the only family left in the waiting area. Finally, the circulating surgical RN called all of us into the conference room to talk with the chief surgeon.

He looked utterly exhausted yet talked with us patiently, answering all questions, calming the nagging fear. I then realized he had operated for sixteen hours straight. When I asked him how he was able to accomplish this feat, he responded by saying a bomb could have gone off next to him and he would have never heard it as he dissected one millimeter at a time. I will never forget his exhaustion, skill, and the depth of his kindness and sensitivity.

Post-Mother of All Surgeries

Brady

After the sixteen-hour surgery, I was taken to recovery, and I began to come out of anesthesia. The epidural had not taken. There was pain that I cannot begin to describe. The pain team, about four or five people, came in and were all over me. They began to administer morphine and I'm not sure what else to get my pain under control. They put ice on my abdomen to determine where I could feel it on my skin, so the providers could then determine where the epidural had not worked. The pain team worked feverishly to bring down the pain level, and upon some relief, I expressed many thanks to them.

The pain simmered down, and I lay there trying to come out of it. Then I remembered that there was the possibility of two stoma.

My hands were on my chest, and I lay there trying to get the courage to reach down and see if I had these bags attached to me and whether or not I still had my bladder or colon. I didn't have the courage to do it. I do not know how long I lay there, but it seemed an eternity.

I was also told there could be some neurological damage, and that it could result in some partial paralysis in my lower legs. Somehow, I was not as reluctant to check for paralysis or weakness. I began to look down at my feet to see if they were moving, but I wasn't sure. I tried to raise my head.

I wanted to see if I could move my feet and lower legs, but I discovered that if you try to move any muscles in your body, you use your stomach muscles! The pain! During the surgery, I was opened up from the sternum all the way down, and my body was stretched completely open—a lot of trauma to the abdomen muscles! It seemed as if I would suffer horrible pain if I just blinked. But I saw my feet moving! Okay, no paralysis! No nerve damage, so that was good. But I was lying there still trying to get the courage to see if I had the stoma. Dr. Walsh then came in to tell me that the surgery went well and that I did not have stomas. He told me that they were able to remove the tumor without having to remove the colon or the bladder. I was relieved. I was in and out of consciousness for a while after the relief of being able to move my legs and the knowledge that I had my colon and bladder.

The next thing I knew, I was moved to a recovery bay. There were different levels of recovery. I was first in immediate recovery, and then went to the recovery bay. I didn't realize it, but as they were wheeling me into the recovery bay, I went right by Beth, Kristopher, Kara, and Shari. I was half conscious and did not know where I was, and suddenly I heard Beth's voice, saying, "Baby!" and I raised my hand. How wonderful it was to hear her voice!

Kristopher

I was so amazed that Brady had the strength and awareness to wave at us as he was wheeled to recovery that I almost didn't believe it when I saw it. I asked him about it later and was amazed all over again when he remembered and confirmed it.

Brady

I had a tube up my nose that went down to my stomach. The primary reason for this is that my stomach needed to be kept empty; if even saliva went into the bowels, the bowels would shut down during surgery. Anesthesia paralyzes the bowels; I assume so that their movement does not interfere with the work of the surgeon. I had IVs. I was catheterized and had a drainage tube in the right side of my abdomen. At the end of the tube was a device that looked like a ball, which drew out fluids. In the first few days after surgery, it was full of blood, but then it shifted to clear liquid with just a little blood.

In the first few days after surgery, the main issue for me was dealing with the pain. I had a morphine drip with a little button on it. When the light went on, it meant that I could push the button and administer the morphine to myself. What a help! It was wonderful to have Beth and the kids there. Beth would rub my arm; Kristopher and Kara would rub my legs. The recovery nurse finally told my family that they had to go and that I needed to rest. I didn't want them to go, but as soon as they left, I went to sleep in about fifteen seconds.

Kara

One of my most vivid memories from the days postsurgery was watching the pain-management team attempt to ease Brady's visible and significant pain. This was the most vulnerable I had seen him and the most helpless we had felt. It was the first time I began to comprehend the complications around this level of pain management.

Brady

I was moved from recovery into a regular hospital room. The nasogastric tube (NG)—the thin tube placed in the nose and leading to the stomach—was removed, but I was still catheterized and had a lot of tubes in me. It was within the first day that a nurse came in, helped me get out of bed, and gave me a sponge bath. It was the second day that I was supposed to get up and start walking around, which was really quite difficult. I had an IV "tree" with several different IV bags. I had the catheter, the drainage tube to the "ball," the receptacle for urine, and the fluid IV. Beth walked with me in small circles around the nurses' station. The first few days were trying to deal with pain, recovering, getting up, and trying to walk—and hoping that my bowels would start to work or "wake up." I could not even drink water at this point but was able to swab my mouth with a sponge; I couldn't swallow even a drip of water from the sponge.

Dr. Pollack came in to check on me, along with two surgical fellows. I prayed, read, and engaged in a great deal of reflection during this time. Soon, I was able to drink water and began doing respiratory exercises. I was starting to feel a little bit better, starting to go on slightly longer walks around the nurses' station. After about seven or eight days, I was able to have my first meal. Beth slept in a chair in my room the first several nights, but as I became more able to walk and eat, she began to sleep back in our room at the Rotary House.

The surgeons and fellows then began discussing discharge. The process before discharge would involve removing the drainage tube, the catheter, and the other IVs. I would then move to the Rotary House, where Beth was staying; it was connected via the skybridge to the hospital and clinic. The plan was for me to stay at the Rotary House for a few days and nights to regain strength for the trip back to Phoenix.

Shari

Brady's recovery exceeded all expectations. He had a few postoperative challenges but nothing that was unexpected for an extremely difficult operative case. Kristopher, Kara, and I returned home to work and continue our ongoing lives. Our worlds had been temporarily suspended in the waiting room and corridors of MD Anderson Cancer Center. Brady had survived, and we had all witnessed a great deal of suffering and a great deal of healing. We were joyous as we jumped on our planes and returned home. Brady was alive, and we were hopeful for his future.

DEATH

Anticipating my discharge with great enthusiasm, Beth went back to the Rotary House and left to do a few errands, getting toiletries and other items necessary for my return to the hotel room. Beth was gone maybe fifteen minutes. I was lying in bed, and suddenly there was pain in my left side. It started strong and then became extreme; there are no words to describe it. The pain was beyond comprehension and any words. I almost lost consciousness. I immediately started perspiring, got cold and clammy, and pushed the nurses' button. I told them, "I'm in trouble." I pulled the sheet over and up and looked at the drainage bag; it was full of blood. I remember thinking, *Uh-oh*. It felt like five or six people had taken a hot poker, stuck it into my abdomen, and were turning it.

By the time the nurses came, I was in shock. My blood pressure was falling rapidly. I could not stop shaking, and I was suddenly as weak as a kitten. Within moments, the room was full of nurses and doctors. I heard someone screaming; it sounded like they were in such agony. When I asked Beth later who the screaming man was, she said that there was no other man…it was me.

Dr. Pollack was unavailable at the time, but Dr. Garcia, one of his fellows, was there. My pulse was weakening. The doctors started to guess what was happening and called the intensive care unit (ICU). Just as all this was happening, Beth walked in the door.

Beth

I walked into Brady's room to see a room full of doctors and nurses and Brady in severe pain. I couldn't believe what I was seeing… When I had left, he was fine. We were supposed to be going to the hotel and then home! What was happening?

My legs were weak. I quickly swallowed an anti-anxiety pill and immediately went to Brady's bedside. I started crying when I saw the tube full of blood. Brady asked me to pray. He was bleeding out, and I couldn't talk. Brady became nauseated and vomited, and my crying was overwhelming. I could not think or talk or pray, only look at him and cry. ICU rushed in with a cart, and a sweet nurse grabbed me and started to pray. "Jesus, please help. Oh, Jesus, please help!" She sat with me in a chair and held me and kept praying out loud while I cried. I didn't know where they had taken Brady.

After what seemed like an eternity, the prayers and the anti-anxiety pill gave me strength, and with the nurse's help, I went up to the ICU floor. I did not know what was happening to Brady but knew it couldn't be good. I started calling family members. I started with Brady's parents and told them something was drastically wrong and would they please pray. I then called my mom, my sister Shari, and my children to tell them, and asked them all to pray. I called our good friend and realtor who was keeping our dogs, Carol, and let her know that Brady was in ICU. Carol said she would continue to take great care of our sweet dogs. After making all the phone calls, I called Brady's parents again to report in. Mary Wilson, Brady's mom, said, "Oh, honey, Dad and I prayed, and an incredible peace came over me! Everything will be okay." I was relieved, amazed, but still scared.

Shari

Beth phoned me about postop day ten. I was between patients and able to take the phone call. Beth was so excited; she was going back to the room to take a shower and do her hair and makeup. The female beautification process was in full swing to welcome her love—her husband—back to the hotel attached to the hospital. The plan was to have Brady transfer to the hotel with daily visits to their outpatient clinic for another week. The goal was to further convalesce until released to fly from Houston to Phoenix. There was a collective sigh of relief and hope. But a few hours later, I received another phone call from my sister. This time it was clear to my staff that it was an emergency, and they hurried me back to my office.

I grabbed the phone to hear my sister screaming and crying, "There's something wrong. There's something wrong with Brady." I could hear a familiar set of sounds in the background—the sounds of hospital staff working through a critical patient who was decompensating rapidly. It had to be Brady's hospital room. I intuitively knew from the very few words that she spoke that Brady was in grave danger. I could hear the tense orders being called out during a code: "I need another line, I cannot get a line!" The language was fast and pressured. The only sound besides Beth's crying were the commands, and I knew that Brady was in trouble.

I asked Beth, "What is going on? Tell me what you're seeing." She couldn't. I said, "Who's with you?" She gave the phone to someone in the room with her, and this woman told me Brady was being moved to critical care and that his vital signs were falling rapidly. I told Beth to move away from the trauma team and let them do their work. I told her I would be there as soon as possible. I was shocked and shaken. My staff was so wonderful. One employee, a nurse, came home with me and helped me pack. Another was on the phone making a plane reservation for me. Within probably two and a half hours, I was on a plane to Houston.

Kristopher

It was a total shock to hear that something quite serious had happened so suddenly. I had just come back from Houston, and by all accounts, Brady was on the road to recovering from this tremendous ordeal. He was stable and in good spirits when I left (although obviously weak and exhausted). It just didn't seem possible that he could get through all that and then be taken down by some kind of unspecified and unanticipated emergency. Although life is unfair and nothing is guaranteed, I remember thinking that he must get through this since he had suffered so much already and gotten through the mother of all surgeries. That must count for something.

We all hoped and prayed again, as everyone had done so much in the past months.

Kara

How quickly things went from optimistic to chaotic. I was in my office, working as a summer associate at a large law firm, when Mom called with the news. I sat in my office and cried, feeling disbelief and dread, helpless to do anything other than hope and pray.

Shari

I did not call my sister from the airport or plane. I did not want to know if he had died until I could arrive and be with my sister. I needed the hope that it was going to be okay. I grabbed a taxi at the Houston airport and told the cab driver in broken sentences, "MD Anderson Cancer Center. Brother-in-law coding. Very serious." There was very little conversation. This intuitive taxi driver just said, "Yes, I will take you there."

I clearly remember the taxi ride. It was bright and sunny, and I prepared for the next bolt of reality. I thought about how much I loved Brady and how much I loved the way Brady loved Beth. Right there in that moment, their love for each other was very much palpable. I just continued to hope Brady was still alive.

The taxi driver interrupted my thoughts with the question, "What entrance do you want to go to?"

I responded, "I have no idea. Since he's so critical, I have no idea where he is."

He replied, "Other people that have been in this situation, I take them to this entrance." I got out of the taxi but didn't recognize where I was at all. I did not want to call my sister, so I just walked in and went up an elevator to an area marked Critical Care. When the elevator doors opened, I looked to my right, and there, standing in front of a window streaming with light, was my sister. No words were needed between sisters at this time.

Intensive Care Unit (ICU)

Brady

Two very athletic young men came to rush me to the ICU. I remember their kind voices, the voices of confident young men encouraging me that I would be okay. They ran me through the halls, hesitating only to wait for the elevator door. The pain caused nausea. I had thrown up earlier, and when the nausea came again, one of the young men very gently turned my head while running down the hallway, so that I wouldn't aspirate on my vomit.

I got into ICU, and they moved me onto a "slab" attached to the wall. My eyes were closed; the lights were bright, and all I could see was red through my closed eyelids. The ICU doctor was by my head and to my left as I lay on the table. He was like a ship's captain, shouting out orders. Also on my left was someone, I think a male nurse, who was taking my blood pressure and reading it out loud. There were six teams of two, so there were twelve people around me trying to get IVs into me. There was a female nurse to the right by my head who asked me what seemed like irrelevant questions: Where was I from? What was the name of the doctor who had placed the port? Was my wife there with me? Did I have any children? At the time, I did not know why she kept asking me these questions, but now, it seems like it was to keep me there and engaged.

I had bled out so much that my veins had collapsed. The teams around me couldn't place IVs in order to get blood into me. A surgical fellow came in and told me that they could not get blood into me, so they had to "cut me down" in order to get access to the femoral artery. They couldn't use any kind of anesthesia because my blood pressure was plummeting. Small incisions had to be made on either side of the groin to access veins. I could hear the nurse shouting out my blood pressure, which was rapidly decreasing…going down, down, down. And then the nurse started talking about having a hard time getting a pulse. Everyone in the room was in control, especially the "captain," who was shouting orders—I had so much confidence in him.

40

As I lay there, I felt the presence of someone walking around me. I did not know who it was, but I *knew* someone was walking *around* me. And then I felt a touch on my knee, then my elbow, then my shoulder, my forehead, and again on the other side of me—my knee, my elbow, and my shoulder. I heard a female voice say, *It's going to be all right, sweetheart.* It was a beautiful voice, a loving voice, a voice so certain that I immediately trusted it. I gave myself to it.

Immediately, I felt calm. I just felt calm that she was there. She walked around the "slab" that I was lying on built into the wall—no one could have walked around it; there were twelve people around and almost on top of me. There was no room for anyone to get in and touch me. But she was there. And I felt calm. Though there was a commanding voice from the ICU physician and the discipline of trained hands all around, there was a frenzied urgency that I sensed in everyone around me. Yet I was calm.

And then everything went black. The lights went away. I could still hear voices. I could hear the nurse saying he could not get a pulse. I could hear orders continuing to be made. Everything was black, and it occurred to me that I could be dying.

Then I could not hear anything at all. I knew immediately, *immediately*, that I was dying, and I was at peace.

Letting God

Dead. That does not describe what it was that I was. True, my blood pressure went to zero. There was no pulse; I was not breathing; my heart had stopped. In my medical record, it states that I had to be revived twice. But I still existed. The "I" that I am existed. Truly, this experience is the most taxing of all my experiences to address in writing. As Emerson states, "My words do not carry its august sense; they fall short and cold."[3] Yet I will attempt to relate to you what the experience was like, for this is the whole point of this writing, of this storytelling. This may be the entire reason I am here.

---

[3] Ralph Waldo Emerson, *The Writings of Ralph Waldo Emerson* (New York: Random House, 1940).

As I noted at the beginning of this story, I have been guided, and my life has been enriched by the writings of men and women who have a gift of language and words that I don't possess. I will rely upon them in my attempt to relate to you what my experience was.

In researching the experiences of other people who have had near-death experiences, or who have coded (died) and then been revived, I found several things in common. One of those things that our words do not capture, in any true way, *is* the experience. Every narrator of his or her story is met with feelings of frustration and incompleteness in their attempt to communicate the experience to others using our common language.

I won't say that I was surprised by what followed. It would require emotion to be surprised, or at least common emotion. But everything that followed fell into place as one unexpected occurrence after another. As Emerson notes, "As a wise old proverb says, 'God comes to see us without bell.'"[3] There is no membrane that separates one from God in these matters. It was from this experience that I feel I came to truly understand the I-Thou.

Martin Buber[4] brilliantly wrote of this. The thing that we are sees the world as a series of things; what Buber calls the "it" as opposed to the "Thou." Indeed, the ego mind that we are sees ourselves as a thing or object. We call ourselves by our role (husband, wife, father, mother, son, daughter), our profession, our race, our religion, our politics. All these "things" can define us and others as the things that we are. They are, as Owen Barfield states, a "world of outsides with no insides to them,"[5] a brittle surface world, an object world in which we ourselves are mere objects. But the soul that we are, the "I," is absent ego. It is the I that exists in the presence and as a proximate result of the "Thou."

I am referring to the "I" as the sacred soul. That being what Emerson describes as "the soul of the whole; the wise silence; the

---

4   Martin Buber, *I and Thou* (trans. Walter Kaufmann) (New York: Charles Scribner's Sons, 1970).
5   Albert Linderman, *Why the World around You Isn't as It Appears: A Study of Owen Barfield* (Barrington, MA: Lindisfarne Books, 2012).

universal beauty, to which every part and every particle is equally related; the eternal ONE."[3] And I am referring to the "Thou" as God.

There is no separation. There is a fidelity between the creator and the created; the object and the subject are one. As for my certainty of it, Emerson may have said it best: "How do you know it is the truth, and not an error of your own? We know the truth when we see it, from opinion, as we know when we are awake that we are awake."[3] *You just know.*

And so, what I am about to write, I write because "I know." And this "knowing" is much like what I and others like me feel when having such an experience. Research on people who have death experiences indicates that we come to know whatever it is that we are made to know without words. Instead, it is as I have described: "you are made to know" whatever it is that you are made to know.

If my experience was ordered in some sequence, the first thing I was made to know was that all was well with my soul. Again, if human emotions were part of my experience, this would have evoked surprise. But I was not surprised. I was humbled. Please don't take "humbled" to mean an emotional state like being shamed or degraded. Rather, it was the independence of being freed from the restrictions and delusions of the ego. I was stripped of all pretentions so that I existed there just as did the Thou, God. I will repeat that: I existed there just as did God; there was no separation. Just as God is the I Am, so was I at that moment; stripped of every "thing," I was in the presence of the I Am.

I experienced grace, I experienced forgiveness, I experienced being embraced. I was drawn into direct experience with God. I was now the "I" of the "I-Thou." There was no separation between the I that I was and the Thou—between God and me. Not only was I acutely aware of the relationship between me and God, I was lost in the relationship, being without ego. I "resided" in and amid this region, or realm of experience, from which all meaning originated. I knew this was the haven of soul.

I knew that all was known about me, and that God knew all there was to know about me. This was a kind of review of my life, all of it. And, upon review, there was no good and bad, no right and wrong. These were simply the facts, the elements, the pieces of my life before me. This was a picture of the thing that I was. But it was secondary at best. What was of utmost importance before me was the soul that I am. The sacred relation to God that had resided in me just before leaving the inanimate body that was resting in the ICU at MD Anderson Cancer Center in Houston. And now, the soul that I am resided not just with God but shared a relationship with God. This relationship, indistinguishable from the I or the Thou, is, I am certain, the ultimate and last "place" for each of us.

This "review," which was exhaustively known by both me and God, seemed a kind of judgment. There was no conclusion, no discernment, no opinion, no assessment. There was only the history of my life here on earth being dragged out into the light. And the light, though it was shown on me, flashed from me so that I knew who it was that I truly was.

The darkness around me was not foreboding. I had no dread of it. Rather, it was restful, peaceful. While experiencing this "place," I experienced a sense of peace that I cannot articulate. There was an atmosphere of peace and love that was so pervasive that I could not, upon reflection, distinguish myself from it. It was the "peace of God, which surpasses all understanding."[6]

I was there as the I that I can recount, but there was no self-awareness. I had no sense of myself as distinguished from or apart from all that I was experiencing at the moment. These words are but a reflection on a past and have been assigned to the experience in my effort to relay it. I hope that you may understand some part of it.

I have said to my family and others that my experience was as if I were in a holding place. Like getting to the symphony late and having to wait outside where you can only hear a hint of the music, I was not yet fully at my destination. As indescribable as the peace and love I experienced were, I knew that it was so much richer if I had "moved on." There are no words in any language to describe what I experienced. However, if I had to try, it was like being just outside

---

[6] Philippians 4:7 from the Holy Bible.

magnificent music; I could feel it, but I couldn't go in to hear it. I did see a bright white light way ahead but did not get to it.

It was here that I was made to know that I could return. Being of no ego at this point, there was a moment, an instant of reorienting to "the person that I am/was." Immediately I knew of Beth, the kids, family, friends, my work, and all that there was to do here. I knew it was for me to return. I was aware of being asked if I was willing to go back. *Willing* is not the right word, because in the absence of ego, there is no will, no willing. It was more like I was being asked if I would submit to going back. I think about the word *suffer* and that it can mean *to allow*. I was made to know that if I would submit, if I would allow it, I had to ask. And, yes, I said yes. Then I prayed, "Dear God, if it is your will, yes, I will go back." Immediately, the lights came back on. I was back in the ICU. I heard the nurse say, "I've got a pulse."

He started reading off my blood pressure. I didn't know how long I was "away." As Byron put it, the soul "can crowd eternity into an hour, or stretch an hour into eternity."[7] My memories were vague in the time after I was revived. It may have been that I was in and out of consciousness. I do not know. The team stabilized me. They used a CT scan to determine the exact location of the bleed. By this time, Dr. Pollack and Dr. Walsh were at the hospital to open me up again. I was being prepared for surgery.

Beth

I was able to see Brady briefly before surgery and after the ICU experience. At that time, I did not know what had happened to him. He had what looked like a space helmet on with a glass front over his face. He was very peaceful and smiled at me; he said, "It's going to be fine." I smiled at him and told him I loved him. I knew he would be okay; Mary, Brady's mom, was very sure he would be all right, especially after the prayer and peace she had received. Brady was lying on

---

[7] George Gordon Byron, *The Works of Lord Byron Complete in One Volume* (London: John Murray, 1840).

the table ready to be wheeled into surgery and the physician/orderly (I'm not sure who it was) told me, "Just want you to know, these surgeries rarely work."

Brady

I went back to surgery. They opened me up and found the source of the bleeding. They had to clean out a lot and then sew me back up...again.

What the doctors think happened was that the extreme loss of blood was from an artery on the left side of the pelvis that had become weak due to the large tumor on the right side of my abdomen that restricted blood flow. When the tumor was removed and blood flow was restored, it formed an aneurysm. When the aneurysm blew, I felt the horribly intense pain. It required fourteen units of blood to stabilize me. I learned later that this was a big deal; I had essentially lost every drop of blood in my body. The blood flowing into my abdomen created the pain, and everything else that I experienced was what happens when you are dying.

When I came to after surgery, I was restrained and intubated. The doctors wanted me to remain semiconscious to be assured I could breathe on my own. I woke up in restraints with my arms stretched out on each side and laid flat on the table. I guess I struggled and tried to pull out the intubation tube, so my arms and legs were restrained. Beth came in and saw me confined in this way with the tube in my throat and asked if there was anything she could do. I grunted and tried to point to the tube down my throat as if to say, "Get these things off me and out of me!"

Of course, she could not have helped me.

Beth

I walked into ICU and saw Brady, his arms out to his side, tied down, and intubated. I felt as if I were in a dream; it was not real, but it was. I didn't cry. I could only look and wonder why he was motioning with his hand toward the tube in his mouth. I was completely numb. Finally, I went to the nurses' station and told them he was having a hard time. A nurse came and sedated him.

Shari

I decided to call Kristopher and Kara. I would give them the option: if they wanted to see Brady, they needed to come now. No one could guarantee that he would be alive in the next five hours. He was very critical. I talked to Kara and gave her the details. I asked her to talk to Kristopher as I needed to be with Beth. Beth and I sat and waited every hour for the next report… He was still alive. As the evening sun fell across the same windows, I told Beth, "We need to go back to the hotel. You need to get rest. We've got another day."

She said, "Nope. Nope. I am not leaving. I'm not leaving." It was clear that she would not leave, and it was not worth the energy to try to convince her to get some rest.

The waiting area in Critical Care was closing. Family and visitors were not allowed to stay in the area overnight. We had to find another place nearby to maintain our vigilance. We went along a hallway and around a corner, and I could actually see into the Critical Care area and the corner of Brady's room. I could see the respirator mechanism going up and down. I pointed this out to Beth, and it convinced her that we were in a good place to sit.

We pulled chairs together to create a makeshift bed. The only way I could get her to lie back in the chair was to tell her we would set an alarm on my phone every hour, get up, and look into his room, make sure the respirator was still engaging Brady's lungs with oxygen. Within minutes, the room got very chilly. It felt like the air conditioner was on full blast. We were getting chilled, and I got up in the large dark room to search for any kind of blanket. Somehow, within seconds, a tall young man with the most gorgeous dark skin walked toward me with four warm blankets and two pillows. He was our angel that night. I can still see his kind eyes in my mind's eye. He still brings peace to me now as I write this.

That was how we spent the night. Every hour, we got up, checked to see if the respirator was still running, and then snuggled back down into our heavenly blankets. A few hours later, I awoke to Kara walking into the waiting area. Beth and Kara were allowed to go back and visit Brady. I took a deep, cleansing breath. He was still alive. After the first twenty-four hours, Brady's vital signs grew more consistently stable. Brady was a fighter and a survivor. The medical team weaned him off the vent with success. When he regained consciousness, it became evident that hypoxia had not caused any cognitive damage. Again, I was so very grateful he had chosen MD Anderson Cancer Center.

Kara

Today, I have no memory of booking a flight, traveling to Houston, or getting to MD Anderson Cancer Center for this second trip, or even flying back to Portland after. My only memory is of sitting in this new, different waiting room with Mom and Shari and visiting Brady in his ICU room. By the time I had arrived, we were just beginning to exhale; we had been holding our collective breath to see if he might survive.

Brady had survived, seemingly to the surprise of everyone. Even with him right in front of us, the episode still seemed surreal. We spoke in hushed whispers in the ICU, as if speaking about his survival out loud might jinx it. The mood didn't feel jittery with anxiety or anticipation; it was simply heavy—with comprehension of what his body had experienced and gratitude that he was still with us.

Brady

After two days, I was taken back up to a hospital room. The nurses had written on the white board, "Welcome back, Mr. Wilson."

I was consumed with the experience and the story after being discharged. I think that due to the pain associated with the experience, my mind was attempting on its own part to repress the experience. I fought against it because the whole encounter was so important to me. So that I might remember it and be able to relate it, I rehearsed it every night. I would go to bed, and before falling asleep,

I would rehearse every facet of it, detail by detail. I considered that there might be skeptics, but I was not concerned with that. If someone didn't understand, I believed that it simply was not yet their time.

Discharge and Home

I was discharged after another week. Beth and I stayed at the Rotary House for a couple of days until we flew home. I had not been eating while I was hospitalized. It was only at the very end of my hospitalization and the two days at the Rotary House that I ventured, very cautiously, to eat again. The day I was discharged, my weight was one eighty due to all the IV fluids pumped into me during my hospital stay. After Beth and I returned home, all the fluids started to drain out of me. Very soon, I looked like a skeleton.

Hope

Within a week to ten days after we returned home, everything in the backyard turned green. The plants came out of it. Beth and I were both stunned. Some leaves dropped, and new leaves took their place. Things started blooming, and two weeks after we returned home, the flowers and shrubs looked as wonderful as they had ever been and just as fragrant. Again, the condition of the plants seemed to reflect my condition. But this time, it was one of healing and restoration, of being redeemed.

An infection had occurred in two places along the incision after the second surgery. The staples that held the incision together had to be removed in our home to dress the wounds. The incision was a little over a foot long, and a nurse would come in to dress the wounds. It was interesting to learn how the wounds healed from the inside out. After we returned home, I needed to learn how to clean the wounds myself. In the morning and evening, I would clean the wounds and apply new dressing to each area. I would remove the gauze while in the shower in the morning and evening, then using surgical gloves, sterile saline, and new sterile gauze, I would "stuff" the dressing back into the wound.

The stent from my right kidney to my bladder moved around in such a way that an end of it was poking into the side of my bladder, causing constant pain. But the stent had to remain in place for six weeks after my surgery, so I had to deal with it. Nevertheless, I was so grateful to be at home with Beth and our children, our granddaughter, our friends, and my clients.

I was eager to get back to activity and work once we arrived home. I was limited at first in doing things at home because I was so weak. I had just spent over two weeks in bed while having my body experience significant trauma. Once I began to gain strength, I still refrained from going out, mostly because my appearance was frightening. I had that skeletal look, accompanied by a pasty appearance. I did not want to shock anyone.

Soon after we arrived home, the whole family came over to visit. Our son, Kristopher, and our granddaughter, Ruby, were there. Ruby wanted to play, which delighted me, but Kristopher was quick to warn her when she wanted to bounce on my stomach. Kara and her future husband, Tyler, were there. When Tyler saw me, he turned to Kara and said, "I wasn't prepared for this."

However, I began to walk more, spend time in my garden, and eventually venture back into my office. I didn't see clients initially, but I did call them and let them know that I would be scheduling soon. I went through mail, recorded a new voicemail for my phone message, and began to prepare my office and myself to resume work. I was eager to go back to work, and I sensed that I was somehow new. What I had experienced had changed me. But the changes were not all clear to me at the time. I was immediately full of gratitude for being given the chance to return to my family, friends, and work. I also felt that I had something new, something else to offer this life, but it wasn't clear to me what it was at the time. I was enthusiastic!

About a month after I returned home, a friend of mine, the one who had written me a check, was having a sixty-fifth birthday. His wife was having a surprise birthday party for him, so Beth and I flew up to Coeur d'Alene, Idaho. I was still struggling with the stent, but

I was grateful to be there, to thank him for all he had done for us, and to tell him my story.

This entire time, I had, of course, been in touch with my parents. About a week and a half after coming home from our friend's birthday, my mom passed away. She had suddenly become ill, and it turned out that she had become septic. She died quickly. It was very hard going to California to tend to my dad and help him with my mom's belongings. Dad asked me to speak at Mom's funeral service. It was difficult to anticipate speaking at a time when I was grieving so much. But I sensed that there was something to be said of Mom's beautiful spirit as well as her current well-being. I loved her very much and missed the sound of her voice. She was a beautiful, sweet woman.

Beth was there with me, as well as Kara and Kristopher. That helped immensely. At her funeral, I spoke of what I was certain was her experience going into this "place" that goes beyond all understanding. I spoke of the beauty that she saw in this world. I spoke of her love.

About two weeks later, Beth and I were sitting on our back porch enjoying the yard and the birds. I was thinking about my mom and reflecting. Beth and I were just quiet. I began to cry; I wished that I'd had one more chance to talk with her. I never had a chance to see her after the surgery, never had a chance to hold her. I was feeling so sad about it.

I talked to Beth about how I was feeling. We were sitting there, and suddenly a breeze came, and it carried the most incredible perfume! I know every flower/plant in our backyard, and *none* smelled like this. The smell of this perfume was incredible and not of this earth. Beth and I both knew it was my mom. We smelled it at the same time. I said, "Mom," and Beth said, "Mary." We both just sat there knowing Mary was present.

What I take from all this is that no matter how much ugliness there is, no matter how much betrayal, no matter how vicious, misguided, or ignorant this world is, there is a promise for every one of us. There is a purpose and a direction. There is a hope for all of us.

We are here to help each other. Every one of us is here to help someone else. There is so much that can be found in that.

In my relationship with Beth, and now in my relationship with what some call God, or however you conceive of God, I have learned something about love that I did not know before. I don't know how to tell anybody about it. But each day, I think I am learning a little bit more about how to show it.

Prostate Cancer

As Emerson stated,

> Our faith comes in moments; our vice is habitual.
> Our being is coming over us from we know not where. This is a universal "sense." To be accompanied at all times by a source unknown.
> The soul requires truth, but truth does not define it.
> The soul requires beauty, but beauty does not define it.
> The soul requires justice, but justice noes not define it.
> When the soul speaks to someone, they immediately become virtuous.[8]

After my 2008 death experience, I was blessed to be alive, working, seeing family and friends. Little did Beth and I expect another cancer "hit," but looking back, it is not surprising.

Many people suffer from different kinds of cancer in the body. In 2014, I was diagnosed with prostate cancer. We knew exactly what to do. I emailed my oncologist, Dr. Deka Araujo, at MD Anderson Cancer Center in Houston. She immediately responded for me to

---

[8] Emerson, *The Writings of Ralph Waldo Emerson* (New York: Random House, 1940).

contact Dr. John Araujo in the Prostate Cancer Center. We made an appointment and headed back to Houston.

Dr. John Araujo was well aware of my situation, past leiomyosarcoma surgery, and ICU experience. Rather remarkably, on the same day we saw Dr. Louis L. Pisters. Dr. Pisters is an excellent surgeon who is usually out of the country, either lecturing or providing help in countries like Africa, but he was in the Urology Cancer Center that day. I was able to see Dr. Pisters immediately, which is generally not the case. I usually made an appointment to return and see the surgeon. Dr. Pisters's subspecialty is performing radical prostatectomies with patients who had previously been treated by invasive procedures, which would cause lesions and scarring and therefore complicate the surgery.

Dr. Pisters met with Beth and me. He was a very kind and caring person in addition to being an excellent surgeon and could see from my medical records my past leiomyosarcoma surgery and the post-ICU surgery. After our meeting with Dr. Pisters, I was facing another surgery, this time to remove my prostate. Dr. Pisters prescribed Lupron, a medication to maintain my PSA at a decreased level. The surgery was successful, and gratefully, the cancer had not spread to my bones or lymph nodes. However, for people who do not have enormous amounts of scar tissue inside their abdomens, a typical prostate removal surgery would be approximately two hours, without encountering any unknowns. Since I had many "fields" of scar tissue and lesions, it took Dr. Pisters approximately seven hours for my prostate surgery.

I have been receiving Lupron injections for almost eight years. This medication (an androgen suppressant therapy) brings the testosterone levels close to zero, which slows the cancer's growth. This medication has been successful until recently (April 2022). A visit to my local urologist indicated that my PSA had now increased to .03—not a great sign.

I have not been able to live up to the death experience, the experience of God, and the remnant of the experience that guides, directs, and comforts me every hour, day, month, year. I was emptied out. I mean the experience of being reduced to the point where I was able, finally, to see beyond myself. I mean the experience of leaving everything behind and at my death, and in it, discovering everything that was really of value.

What is clear to me is that I have changed, that the death experience has changed me through and through in so many ways. But I have the same mind that I had before dying and "being brought to life." The blessing is that I am more aware than I ever was before about the separation, the profound difference between the egoic mind and the soul.

I am accompanied. I experience conscience not as an internalized set of dos and don'ts, not as a set of rights and wrongs. Rather, I am accompanied at all times by direction. And I know that I am doing God's will when I submit to it. I know that prayer is always an act of listening. I know that there is no moment where God is not available for direction. And I know that to live most fully is to submit to the direction that is always there. Of course, I fail. That is what I mean about not living up to the experience. But I know that I have failed when I have. That is the blessing.

As a clinical psychologist, I recognize that every soul that enters my office for help is perfect in every way. My work is with the mind that torments the person who is there searching with me. It is the activity of the egoic mind that drives us, plagues us, misguides us. It does this because it wants to be in control. It functions in such a way as to put us in a kind of sleep state. We think we are awake, but we are actually asleep and dreaming that we are awake. We are not conscious unless or until we hear the soul's calling.

(After I returned to my office and full-time work, I did not want to forget any part of my cancer experiences. I video-taped myself telling my entire story, which took about three hours. Beth then transcribed the words you have read in order to preserve the experience and convey it to you. The poems were added when Beth wrote my story.)

Beth

It was December 2014. Brady had just returned in November of that year from yet another deadly cancer: prostate. However, he was here, alive, having survived yet another extremely difficult surgery. The picture below is in the fall of 2014 after Brady's prostate surgery. I was healthy and very grateful.

With Brady feeling better, we decided it was time to downsize, especially after the second cancer. We had a great house in Scottsdale, where our families gathered on many occasions. It was a tough decision to leave our home, but the best decision at the time.

With our real estate agent, I set out to look for houses. Since Brady's office (and the shared offices of our friends/practice partners of Brady's) were close to where we lived at the time, I looked in the same area so he would not have such a long commute. Brady is a well-known and highly credible clinical and forensic psychologist who had been practicing in Scottsdale for many, many years. We found a smaller home in North Scottsdale that had been remodeled. It had three bedrooms and an office.

As difficult as it was after fifteen years of marriage to start disposing of belongings, we started the process of downsizing. I was home full-time at this point and could devote my time to sorting, packing, and getting the house ready to sell—a feat in its own right. The wonderful memories of our granddaughter learning to swim in our backyard pool; the numerous family gatherings, Christmas, Thanksgiving, birthdays; sitting outside by the pool with our family; and the fire in the terra cotta chiminea at Christmas would be forever in our hearts.

I would also miss Brady's and my walks through a beautiful neighborhood, swimming in our pool, and walking our three dogs—Chip (Brady's golden); Fremont (a Shih Tzu), my children's (and my) dog from my first marriage in Michigan; and Zoe, a dog I rescued from a horrible pound in Anderson, Indiana. When Fremont got older, Brady would put him in a kids' front pack so he could go on the dog walks. We loved our dogs; they were part of the memories in our home.

My Previous Life

I left my ex-husband in 1992. My children and I moved to Anderson, Indiana, where my mom, my sister, and her family lived. Fortunately, I had received my PhD from Michigan State University, where I had a teaching and research assistantship. Prior to moving to Indiana, I was hired at Western Michigan University, where I taught for a year. I had plenty of experience in teaching college students and doing my own writing and publishing in peer-reviewed academic journals. I contacted Ball State University, only twenty-five minutes or so from our home in Anderson, and began my seven-year career there (I was tenured at Ball State University, the year Brady and I were married, and I moved to Arizona). I loved my discipline, and I loved teaching upper undergraduate and master's level courses. The students were wonderful, and many were first-time college students in their families. What a joy to help them in their own journeys.

The first year in Indiana, my daughter and I lived with my mom, who cooked for us, rubbed our backs at night—took care of us. My son (seven years older than my daughter—same father) lived on the other side of town with my sister and her family. Her eldest son was the same age as my son (first cousins); they were great friends. My ex-husband, our children, and I had always spent holidays with my family in Indiana, or my family was in Michigan with us.

I knew I needed to find a house in Anderson and establish a home for my children, me, and, of course, Fremont. I found a house about five minutes from my sister and her family that was also close to a grade school for my daughter. My sister's youngest son, who was only two years younger than my daughter (first cousins), walked to and from school together and would often bring friends back to our house. It really felt like home.

It was the first Christmas in our own Anderson home. My son and daughter, my mom, my sister and her family, and another divorced friend and her daughter were all there. When everyone was gone, the house quiet, both of my children in their own room, I was lying in my bed and breathed a huge sigh of relief and thanks. I was wide awake, thinking about the day. Lying in my bed and on my back, I could see the end of the hallway that led to my children's bedrooms.

Quite suddenly, I saw a white, round "thing," almost like an orb, at the end of the hallway, moving into my room. I blinked several times to make sure I was awake—I was. The "orb" moved to the end of my bed and became a white cross. It stayed for a few minutes and then dissipated. I thought my heart was going to jump out of my chest—it raced profoundly! Could this have been real? It was. I was a bit shaken, but absolutely amazed and excited! I had a couple of incredible spiritual experiences in Michigan, but this one was *indescribable and extremely powerful.*

Mom helped me a great deal to furnish the house (she was a wonderful pastor's wife during my dad's ministry in Michigan—and also should have been an interior designer). My dad (master's in theology from Oberlin) had a wonderful ministry in our church in St. Joseph, Michigan. Mom was the consummate pastor's wife, having people from our church over to our home for church board/committee meetings and otherwise—and for dinners (tons of dinners: she always cooked and was great at it; I didn't get the good-cook gene). She counseled people from the church on many, many phone calls. My parents and our family were loved, and we loved the people in our church, who were so very good to us.

As a pastor's kid, I was raised by parents who were liberal, critical thinkers; they were the only white people who supported civil rights in our primarily white, Southwestern Lake Michigan town in the 1960s. Dad was the only white person to march for Civil Rights in Benton Harbor, Michigan—home to more African Americans than our white town, which had only one African American family. I had good roots in *real* Christianity, i.e., forgiveness (forgiveness is of the heart—we are not to live in abusive situations and must have personal boundaries); absolute nonprejudice against any person from a "different" race, ethnicity, or religion; grace, kindness, empathy, and care for those less fortunate. In other words, the Way of Jesus (Yeshua).

I am extremely thankful to my parents for beautiful church services that were *never* fearful, *never* spoke of punishment, and were always full of love. I always had faith, but I questioned it, of course, like most people. One of Dad's favorite sayings was, "Honest doubt is better than pretended belief." That *always* stuck with me. I distinctly remember Mom and Dad, and my sister and me (in grade school at the time) sitting in front of the fireplace in our home on a very, very cold Michigan winter's night. As we watched the fire and talked, Dad said, "See those logs burning? They don't die, they just change form." That *always* stuck with me too. These were wonderful memories of my previous life.

As Brady mentioned in his journey, our parents were neighbors and good friends before we were born. My mom and Brady's mom kept in touch over the years. Brady's parents lived in California, and my mom (and dad before his death) in Indiana. Brady came with a friend to Michigan when I was sixteen; he was twenty-one. We went to the Lake Michigan beach in our town and walked together. Needless to say, sparks flew. However, Brady went on with his life, and I went on with mine. After I had been divorced for seven years and living in Indiana, Mom called me to say that she had talked with Mary (Brady's mom) and learned that Brady was also divorced. That next summer, Brady came to the hometown in Indiana for a golf tournament, invited by a childhood friend. We re-met that summer, and two years later, we were married. We have always known that a marriage would not have worked for us prior to that moment. The timing was right.

Fast-forward to fifteen years of marriage, and after his two cancer surgeries in 2008 and 2014, it was my turn to suffer.

March 2015
Scottsdale, Arizona

Brady and I made the move to the downsized house. Since the house was smaller, we had to buy new den furniture, a small high-top table for the kitchen, and several other items, but we made it work, and it was fine. We felt blessed to have been able to find a place we could afford, still relatively close to Brady's office.

It was around June of 2015. I started feeling physically awful. I had never felt so full of pain—everywhere in my body. Until this point, I had great energy. I loved taking my granddaughter to movies and out for sushi—her favorite. It was highly unusual for me to feel this bad; I had been very active my entire life—always exercising, working, walking dogs. My pain grew so bad all I could do was lie in bed.

Acupuncture had worked for me in the past for lower backaches. I went back to a highly reputable acupuncturist in Tempe, Arizona, who had helped me several years previous. When I returned home that day, I started shaking. My entire body was shaking, and I could not stop. Never had I experienced anything like that. It was the weekend, so I waited until Monday, and Brady called our primary care doctor, a wonderful practitioner, who suggested clonazepam to calm my shaking; it helped. I was still shaking, but just not as crazy as before taking clonazepam.

This started my three-year research into what was wrong with me. I started having periods of feeling like I was going to faint if I tried to get up, and I felt nauseated. I was extremely weak and many times very dizzy. Brady and I decided I should go back to a trusted orthopedic physician/surgeon, because we did not know what else to do. My husband and I had counted on his diagnoses for years. He told me he didn't know what was wrong with me (he was so honest), which we really appreciated, but we were back to square one.

The horrendous pain in my head, neck, and abdomen, plus the weakness and lightheadedness, was more than I could bear, and Brady took me back to our primary care physician, who had moved on to another practice. She ordered an MRI of my cervical spine, which indicated that my facets from C2 to C7 were normal for my age. She also ordered an ultrasound of my abdomen. My liver was normal, my gallbladder indicated no stones or bile-duct dilation, pancreas and spleen were normal, kidneys were normal, my aorta was normal, and there was no free fluid. Results: a negative abdominal ultrasound.

My primary care physician then recommended that I see a local neurologist, which I did. The neurologist examined me, and I pointed out a very slight tremor in my neck. He said that it was essential tremor and benign. The neurologist ordered imaging of my chest; the results indicated a small left pleural effusion, but that did not explain my symptoms. One month later, due to my severe pain, my husband and I went back to the same neurologist to see if there was another test. He ordered an angiogram that indicated no intracranial aneurysm. So, essentially, no answer for the intense head, neck, and body pain.

Brady had to drive me everywhere, and that really impacted his clinical practice, which was not good. I had to get well. One evening, I was so bad that Brady took me to the emergency room at a local hospital. I was tremoring and, of course, in a great deal of pain, and after waiting quite a while, I was finally in a room. A nurse came in and, somewhat impatiently, asked why I didn't call my neurologist.

I was in too much pain to answer, and she asked me if anyone in my family had Parkinson's disease, which my maternal grandfather did have. The nurse asked me if I wanted a Xanax, which I declined. The emergency room then dismissed me.

Not getting any answers, I lay in our bed and kept researching on my phone. I started finding some interesting possibilities that had not been mentioned by my providers. One of the interesting possibilities that might be connected to my intense pain, fatigue, nausea, weight loss, and intense loss of energy is expanded on below.

Methylenetetrahydrofolate Reductase (MTHFR)

Methylenetetrahydrofolate reductase (MTHFR) is a genetic mutation that leads to high homocysteine levels in the blood. Homocysteine is a chemical in the blood, "formed when the amino acid, methionine, which is a building block of the proteins in our food and body, is naturally broken down (i.e., metabolized) to be excreted in the urine." For this recycling, I needed vitamins B_{12}, B_6, and *folate*, not folic acid. "If a person is deficient in vitamin B_{12}, B_6, or folate, homocysteine cannot be efficiently recycled and therefore accumulates in the blood."[9]

Unfortunately: "The US Preventive Services Task Force and the American Academy of Family Physicians have both concluded that there is insufficient evidence to screen asymptomatic adults (for MTHFR) with no history of coronary heart disease to prevent coronary heart disease." Obviously, more research needed to be conducted on children and adults regarding the impact of high levels of homocysteine (it is an easy blood test at your provider's office/lab). How many people know about the MTHFR gene mutation? My guess is not many.

I immediately tested for the MTHFR gene mutation. I had it. Good to know. I started on a multivitamin with folate, B_{12}, and B_6.

---

[9] S. Moll and E. A. Varga, "Homocysteine and MTHFR mutations," *Circulation* (2015), 132(1), https://www. ahajournals. org/doi/full/10. 1161/ CIRCULATIONAHA. 114. 013311.

Many people with mystery illnesses may have this genetic mutation. The gene mutation can be heterozygous or homozygous. As I had found in my research, "[s]ome people have a genetic mutation in one or both of their MTHFR genes. People with a mutation in one MTHFR gene are said to be heterozygous; if mutations are present in both genes, the person is said to be homozygous or compound heterozygous for the mutation(s)."[9]

Since Mom and Dad both passed due to heart problems (Mom had congestive heart failure, and Dad had a massive heart attack), it would have been reasonable for me to be tested for the MTHFR gene mutation. However, it was my own research while lying sick in bed that led me to get tested. I am acutely aware of the massive patient overload for primary care physicians, physician assistants, and nurse practitioners. However, if a patient has parental/genetic history of heart problems, shouldn't that patient be tested? There are possibilities for many diseases based on this genetic mutation, yet MTHFR testing has not been advised.

Back to my detective work. Trying to follow every possible lead, Brady drove me to a physician who specialized in neurological diseases like Parkinson's, Huntington's, tremor disorders, and similar conditions. I was tested using electromyography (EMG), which is used to diagnose nerve and muscle disorders (definitely not a fun procedure). I spent several hours with the physician who tested me for cognitive problems, balance issues, and the EMG. Nothing was found to be wrong. He took my physical problems very seriously.

My primary care physician then suggested that I go to a physiatrist. Without seeing me or talking to me, the physiatrist came into the room and said he had looked at my X-ray and there was nothing wrong with me. The tone of his voice and nonverbal communication was extremely rude and disbelieving of my pain. Many people have been told their symptoms were "in their head." There are far too many stories like this—of providers dismissing distressing symptoms because they don't know what is wrong and were not taught about it in medical school.

During visits with my primary care physician, there was a small amount of blood found in my urine, so she recommended a visit with a urologist, which I did. I had a bladder ultrasound. The results indicated "no bladder calculi or masses." I had many visits to our orthopedic physician/surgeon for neck cervical scans/X-rays, lower-back scans, and more X-rays. Before I became sick, he ordered physical therapy, which always seemed to help me. However, after becoming ill, I did not have the stamina and was entirely too weak to do physical therapy.

The previous physician visits, testing, and exams were done in 2015. In 2016, I called my gastroenterologist and went in to see the physician assistant. She ordered a CT of my abdomen and pelvis. Bowel, liver, gallbladder, spleen, and my abdominal aorta were all normal, with no enlarged lymph nodes. "Mild diffuse disc bulges at L 3-4, L 4-5, and L5-S1." The impression by the radiologist was, "No acute findings to explain reported presentation."

Feeling extremely discouraged, still in horrendous pain and unable to sleep, my husband remembered that a colleague had heard of a new female neurologist in Phoenix whom I should try to see. We made an appointment, and she examined me and ordered an MRI of my brain. There was no evidence of "intracranial abnormality." She wanted to try Botox in my head. I agreed and was extremely sick for three weeks afterward. She diagnosed me with cervical dystonia. After seeing her for a few months, she said she did not know what to do and recommended pain management.

Where was God? The incredible spiritual experience that I had in which I saw a white cross at the end of my bed...where was He/She/the Spirit now? I was so mad. I felt betrayed, and had nothing but anger and pain.

During the next two years, I spent 90 percent of my time in bed, in pain. The remainder of the time, I hobbled (with a cane) out to the kitchen to try and find something to eat. My appetite was not good, but I tried to eat carefully, avoiding sweets, sodas, and wheat; I drank rice milk. I took showers when I could. I was scared and getting very depressed. After taking a shower and washing my hair, I was completely and totally exhausted. I had to sit down to dry my hair and then went directly to bed for the remainder of the day. My amazing husband cooked dinners for us during my entire illness (and still does) after his long days with clients. He was and is wonderful—a strong person, both physically and emotionally, after all that he has been through.

I started procedures with the pain-management clinic in December 2016 through February 2018. The diagnoses ranged from spondylosis, atypical face pain, and chronic pain syndrome. I had many procedures using Traumeel (I cannot take steroids) via trigger-point injections or some other type of procedure. Immediately afterward in recovery, I had decreased pain. However, by the time my husband and I left the parking lot, the effect of the medication faded, and the pain returned. You might be wondering why I kept going to pain management when it didn't seem to help. Me too. My only response is that I didn't know what else to do and kept hoping that at some point the procedures would help. They did not. During the entirety of 2017, I was still in pain, 90 percent of the time in bed, weak, lightheaded, nauseated, losing weight, and becoming more depressed and anxious.

I was completely discouraged, hopeless, and losing faith. I could not pray. I was mad at God for my feeling of being totally abandoned. Yet, somehow, I found the motivation to do more research on my phone while lying in bed. I found a physician in the Phoenix area, and we went to see him. I was tested via blood samples and was told, "You have a fungus in your blood." Wow. That was new! He had a remedy—doxycycline. I was elated! But he told me, "You will feel worse before you feel better." Okay, I can do this!

I took one doxycycline one day and tried one the next day—*and definitely thought I was going to die*. A herx beyond description. The term *herxing* would become very familiar to me. It is a shortened version of a Jarisch-Herxheimer reaction. What happens is that many toxins are released too quickly, which creates a severe inflammatory response. *Severe* doesn't even attempt to capture what I felt. I could *not* take doxycycline. More depression, more anxiety, more pain; I felt like I was sinking. Also, during this time, as I was standing (with great difficulty) at our master bathroom sink and brushing my hair, it completely broke off. Lots of my hair had fallen into the sink. Yet another indication something was terribly wrong.

About the same time, my primary care physician suggested that I may have temporomandibular joint dysfunction (TMJ), jaw and head pain. She referred me to a dentist who was supposed to be a specialist in this area. This dentist checked my face with a device and indicated I was quite inflamed and did have TMJ. I was fitted with mouth guards for day and night. After several months of working with this dentist, I could not continue due to body/head/neck pain, the commute, and mostly his rude behavior.

After the inflammation found in my face, I wondered if I had a sinus infection in addition to TMJ. I made an appointment with my ear, nose, and throat (ENT) physician, whom I had seen for many years. He ordered a CT scan of my sinuses. The results: "Small amount of debris in the right sphenoid sinus is noted. This could reflect mild acute sinusitis. Otherwise, paranasal sinuses are clear." Additionally, "the mastoid air cells and middle ear cavities were clear." My primary care physician then ordered a mild antibiotic for a sinus infection, which I took very briefly, but it did not help my pain.

In addition to the rude behavior from the previous TMJ health provider, I decided to go to a TMJ dentist very close to home (about five minutes away) so I could drive myself. She had just opened the TMJ side of her dental practice, and I was one of her first patients. This new TMJ dentist noticed my neck tremor, and I had informed her I was in great pain all over my body. Interestingly, in one of my appointments (all cash, and a lot of it; no insurance accepted) she put at least eight tongue depressors between my teeth, and my head tremor seemed to calm down. During several appointments, I was fitted with a day appliance and a night appliance. The day and night mouth guards kept my mouth wide open and the lower jaw pulled forward—every day, every hour, for about a year. Primarily because I didn't know what else to do, I wore the appliances and hoped over time that they would help my head and neck pain. I could also drive myself because it was so close to home and Brady wouldn't miss his clients by having to drive me to yet another healthcare appointment.

The new mouth guards, which kept my mouth open all day, helped for a year or so. The pain decreased. However, after about a year, it all came back. I went to my extremely competent and caring dentist, Dr. Mitchell Cooper[10], in Scottsdale, and he was very surprised when I opened my mouth. He asked, "What happened to your bite?" I told him about the mouth guards, and he became very concerned. He was an advocate for me and told me about Dr. Mandeep Vermani[11], a board-certified TMJ dentist. I made an appointment with her. The previous two TMJ dentists who treated me were not board certified.

I started working with Dr. Vermani, who took X-rays of my open bite. My dentist had years of X-rays of my bite, which was always closed, i.e., I could chew normally. Obviously, the mouth guards given to me by the previous TMJ dentist had ruined my bite and my jaw. I was in more unbearable and constant daily pain. Dr. Vermani worked with me by prescribing and fitting the correct mouth guards. After approximately a year working with Dr. Vermani, Dr. Cooper built up my lower teeth so I could chew. As of this writing, I am still trying not to depend on my new mouthguards from Dr. Vermani, but I still have headaches, temple pain, and very tight muscles in my neck. But I can chew!

All this work on my mouth has taken two years. And I'm still working on it all. The TMJ pain is, of course, in addition to my body pain. If there's blame in this situation, it is the fault of the National TMJ Board and/or Association. According to the TMJ Association, "TMJ is a complex medical condition that involves multiple body systems—cardiovascular, neurological, immunological, digestive, respiratory, endocrine, and musculoskeletal—which contribute to the onset, development and/or persistence of TMJ, as well as influence treatment outcomes. TMJ is linked to several other medical conditions and is more than just a jaw or dental problem."[12] Given the complexity of TMJ, it is very reasonable that *all* TMJ providers be board certified.

Through 2016 and 2017, the cause(s) of my bodily pain were not found. I tried a chiropractor—I had been to a couple of chiro-

---

[10] Of Grayhawk Dental Associates (https://grayhawkdentalscottsdale.com).

[11] Of Arizona TMJ & Pain Center (http://www.arizonatmjpain.com/doctor/).

[12] You can learn more on the website of the TMJ Association, Ltd. (https://tmj. org/).

practors before getting sick and didn't have any reactions. I felt very confident in this chiropractor, who was trained at the same place my nephew and his wife were trained, at Life University.[13] She was very good; however, I herxed after one session with her. I herxed so badly that the chiropractor tried a procedure used with infants, and I herxed after that one as well. My body/head pain was brutal, as was the chronic fatigue.

I was sure that I was dying.

As I researched on my phone while lying in bed, I came across recommendations to "help" chronic pain, such as meditations, breathing, and others. Are they serious? I am dying here, and I am supposed to meditate and concentrate on breathing! I was furious, sick, mad at God/the Divine, especially after what we had been through with Brady's cancers. Still, what else was there to do when you are out of your own resources, no one knows what is wrong with you, you feel like you are dying and can barely hobble to the bathroom only a few feet from the bedroom?

The only thing I could do was to start praying out loud and plead with God. "Where are you? Help me!" I said this over and over while I cried and cried. Barbara Brown Taylor captures how I felt when she wrote,

> Like darkness itself, the dark night of the soul means different things to different people. Some use the phrase to describe the time following a great loss, while others remember it as the time leading up to a difficult decision. Whatever the circumstances, what the stories have in common is their description of a time when the soul was severely tested, often to the point of losing faith, by circumstances beyond all control. No one chose the dark night; the dark night *descends.*

---

[13] Life Alive Chiropractic in Louisville, CO. Dr. Ryan Schrock, my nephew, and his wife, Dr. Andrea Schrock, are both exceptional chiropractors. Learn more at *Life Alive Chiropractic* (www.lifealivechiro.com).

When it does, the reality that troubles the soul
most is the apparent absence of God.[14]

After *many* days of praying, lying in bed, I had two instances
of *pure joy*. There are no words to describe this type of joy. Nothing
comes close—not the birth of my wonderful children, my marriage
to my amazing husband, *nothing*. *The ecstasy of this joy was not of this
world*. It was profound. I remembered Dad and Mom had a little
red card that had these words on it: "Joy is the most infallible sign
of the Presence of God." Wow. As I recalled that little red card, tears
started rolling. I was not alone. God, the Divine, was with me. There
was no assurance of anything other than "I am here." That was all I
knew, and that carried me as I kept experiencing all the pain and not
knowing what was wrong with me.

As I continued in severe pain, I continued praying. One day, as I
was standing in my closet, the words came to my mind, "Be patient."
I *knew* it was the small voice within—God, the Divine, was still with
me. I knew I must be patient, but I can tell you that, honestly, this
was the most difficult time in my life—and I had to be patient. "Be
still and know…"[15]

When are we still and quiet for long periods of time? When are
we at the total end of our resources? How often do we cry out to the
Divine for help? For most of us, me definitely included, I had to try
and solve it, bear it, be strong. For me, I *had* to get to the end of my
resources, *be still*, be in *solitude*, be *silent* for most of the day, in pain,
for years upon end, lying in bed quietly to hear the small "voice"
within.[16] I had been so strong for my husband as we went through
two deadly cancers. I certainly could handle this, right?

---

[14] Barbara Brown Taylor, *Learning to Walk in the Dark* (New York: HarperCollins
Publishers, 2014).

[15] Psalm 46:10 from the Holy Bible.

[16] Our teacher and pastor, Dave Brisbin, talks about our need for stillness,
solitude, silence, and simplicity to begin the journey inward. You can learn
more at the Effect Church's website (theeffect.org).

Wrong. I could not. And when I was at the very, very end of my coping, *and* I accepted my lack of control and anyone and anything being able to help me, I felt the Divine's presence with me.

New Direction

I love research and have always been quite good at it. As I lay in my bed day after day, I used my phone to do more research to see if there was something I was overlooking. The home we moved into had been remodeled. I read about radon and health risks, especially with lung cancer. We then had an expert come into our home to measure radon. He measured several places in the house and found that we did not have radon exposure—that's good, but it did not explain my health problems.

I went afterward to a new primary care provider since my original provider had moved to Africa to work and help people there. I told my new primary care provider that another physician had said I had fungus in my blood. Continuing to look at her computer, she said, "You don't have a fungus in your blood." *She had not tested me for fungus in my blood.*

At about this time, my husband remembered that one of his clients had gone to a physician who had a small clinic south of Tucson, Arizona. In January of 2017, my husband and I drove over three hours south of Phoenix to see Dr. Michael Gray. It was a small, very unassuming clinic, and we waited quite a long time to see him. The wait was usual because he took so much time with each patient. My husband went in with me, and I explained my situation, that nothing had helped, and asked if he could possibly be of help to me. He sent me to a small hospital close to his clinic and ordered *many* lab tests, which was fine. The nurses there knew what he wanted to order and seemed as if they had done it hundreds of times.

Our next visit to Dr. Gray came with some surprising results. Looking over the lab results, he noted that my transforming growth factor (TGF-β 1) was over 11,000. Brady and I had never heard of TGF. Most physicians order an erythrocyte sedimentation SED rate (ESR), which is a measure of the inflammation in the body and can be indicative of infections and autoimmune disorders. I have had SED rates previously in bloodwork while I was sick, *but they were never elevated.*

What is TGF? According to Yang et al., "Among inflammatory and extracellular matrix regulatory cytokines, transforming growth factor-beta (TGF-β 1) stands central, as it possesses both important immunomodulatory and fibrogenic activities, and should be considered a key for understanding inflammation and remodeling processes."[17]According to the many, many Labcorp results that I have had over the years, "the reference range for TGF-β 1 in a healthy population is 867–6662. However, it should be noted that these ranges are obtained from a limited population of apparently healthy adults and are not diagnostic thresholds."[18]

My TGF-β 1 of 11,000 seemed extremely high. Why doesn't a SED rate capture this kind of inflammation? Why didn't C-reactive protein capture the inflammation? I am not a medical scientist, so I don't know. A critical question is: Why aren't all health providers using multiple methods of assessing inflammation?[1] Disregulation of the immune system is highly correlated with inflammation. Perhaps severe inflammation is part of explaining what was wrong with me. I needed a new direction, and this physician provided one.

Dr. Gray prescribed charcoal, as well as vitamin C, alpha lipoic acid (it took me about three months to get to the prescribed dose), and other vitamins. Charcoal is a binder; it was a major factor in clearing toxins from my body *and* one which I could tolerate. Charcoal worked for me. In about three months, my pain level decreased, but not totally. However, I was very grateful for anything that helped my pain.

During the time I was seeing Dr. Gray, I sought medical attention in Phoenix for what I thought was a bladder infection. The phy-

---

[17] Y. C. Yang, et al., "Transforming growth factor-beta1 in inflammatory airway disease: a key for understanding inflammation and remodeling," *Allergy*, 67(10) (2012).

[18] The Labcorp test was developed, and its performance characteristics determined, by Eurofins Viracor. It has not been cleared or approved by the U. S. Food and Drug Administration.

sician ordered labs to make sure, but he gave me an antibiotic, thinking that I knew what a bladder infection felt like, since I'd had them previously in my healthy life. The physician gave me a prescription for an antibiotic, which did not help. I told Dr. Gray that my pain was similar to a bladder infection. He said immediately, "It's interstitial cystitis." I had never heard of it. Likely, most people haven't. The condition occurs more often in women than men and can occur in children too. The cause of interstitial cystitis is unknown. It is often treated with antibiotics; however, interstitial cystitis does not respond to antibiotics. Interstitial cystitis is "a potentially devastating pelvic pain disorder affecting both women and men."[19]

We continued going to Dr. Gray, and after several months, my TGF β 1 started to decline; however, it took a long time. But there was anti-inflammatory progress! I continually said to my husband during the years we lived in the downsized house, "There's something wrong with this house." I was constantly focused on looking around our house for any sign of anything.

An Answer

One day, I found a small "bubble" near the baseboard in our master bath. I had Brady tear off the baseboard—and it was black underneath. By this time, I had done so much research and knew that it was likely toxic mold.

On finding black mold underneath the baseboard, I called our home warranty company and asked for a referral to a remediation company—this was the best contact that I knew. None of our friends had black mold in their home (that they knew of), and I didn't know who else to contact. The remediation company from Phoenix came and tore out the boards in front of the bathtub and nearby in our bathroom—lots of toxic black mold. The remediation company then brought in giant fans and put at least three in our bathroom. What we didn't know at the time was that they were supposed to put plastic

---

[19] I. Marcu et al., "Interstitial cystitis/bladder pain syndrome," *Seminars in Reproductive Medicine*, 36(2) (2018).

up to secure the bathroom area so the toxic mold would not spread around the house. We assumed the remediation company knew what they were doing. Bad assumption, but we wanted to make sure our home warranty company paid for the cost. The toxic mold was spread all over our house.

I knew from my research we needed to do a mold test in the house and contacted Mycometrics, a well-known company that uses the environmental relative moldiness test (ERMI), developed by the Office of Research and Development of the U.S. Environmental Protection Agency. Not surprisingly, there was Stachybotyrs (genus of fungi) found in the house, as well as other toxic molds, such as Aspergillus (genus of fungi). I *did* have a fungus in my blood! I scoured the garage, and behind the cabinets in the garage, there had been a slow hot water leak that also created toxic mold. A Mycometrics report indicated there was toxic mold in both of our cars. And there's more: toxic black mold was also found in the wall behind the dishwasher. We found that out when we moved out of the house and replaced the dishwasher.

We reported our mold findings to Dr. Gray, who told us to get out immediately. On our way home from south of Tucson that evening, the rain was pouring down, I was crying, and Brady was trying to stay together driving as we realized that everything in our house—*all* our furniture, laptops, phones, dishes—*everything* was going to have to go. Oh yes, and all our clothes. We are not wealthy people.

We called our realtor, Lynn, who was extremely concerned. She knew someone who had worked with toxic mold houses, and he recommended a highly reliable remediation company. The representatives from the new remediation company wrote a seventeen-page report on what the first company did wrong.

Why didn't we sue the first remediation company? By the time we found out that they had done the remediation wrong, it was too late. If we went to court, the bad remediation company could have said that toxic mold was blown in by the wind. We didn't have the time or resources to fight it in court. It is very difficult and generally impossible to seek damages for homes with toxic mold that makes people sick.

First, most physicians and primary care providers do not believe that toxic mold is harmful. Second, we would have needed an expert indicating that my illness was, at least in part, due to the toxic mold—obviously, this was not possible. Thousands of people are in the same situation. Many people have landlords who refuse to bear responsibility for toxic mold and subsequent illnesses of renters.

In the middle of losing all our belongings, there was a blessing: our home warranty company paid for over $27,000 worth of costs that the second, competent remediation company corrected so we could sell the house with full disclosure of what had been done.

Our daughter-in-law came over to supervise and contact agencies to take our furniture, clothing, and all items in the house. Brady had to work; he couldn't do it, and I was too sick. Much of our furniture and belongings went to immigrant families who did not have much; we were very glad that from all our loss, others were helped. Any person or agency who took our belongings were *advised many times* that the items were in a house that had toxic mold. We did not want to live with the possibility that someone might get sick from the mold—like I did. Our son took other belongings out to the curb for bulk pickup. Maybe someone benefitted from finding our stuff. We hoped so. We were very thankful for our son and daughter-in-law, who immediately were there to help us, and our daughter and son-in-law, who gave us much-needed financial support.

Leaving

My sister came out to help us when we left our home, and we moved into the Holiday Inn Express with nothing but the clothes on our backs. She went to a local discount store to get something that I could wear and threw away the clothes I was wearing. She went out and bought necessities like toothbrushes, toothpaste, a hair dryer, soap, etc. We lived in the Holiday Inn for two weeks before we moved into an apartment with nothing but the clothes on our backs.

Brady still had to work, of course, and I was so weak that I was in bed all day at the Holiday Inn.

We had to buy two new cars. Brady went to buy two cars on the same day and then threw his clothes away and put new ones on. It was all *nuts*, but because our home warranty company paid for the remediation of the moldy house, thankfully, we had money to buy two cars. We went to visit a new apartment building constructed near Scottsdale Road, close to where we originally lived.

We are fortunate to have very caring friends. One couple, both psychologists who shared the office space with Brady, knew intimately what we were going through. Our friend said that something came to her: it was to set up a GoFundMe for us. We never would have thought of this. My son set it all up, and we were incredibly blessed to have people (some we didn't even know) give to the fund. It gave us enough money to buy cookware, dishes, food, towels, bathroom stuff, sheets, blankets, pillows, and stools for the apartment, so we would not have to eat sitting on the bathtub and toilet. I do not know what we would have done without our immediate and extended family, friends, and the Divine during this time.

The Apartment

For about a year, we lived in a seven-hundred-square-foot apartment with not much but a bed, kitchen stools, and kitchen/bath necessities. We were fortunate. Most people in the world live with less. We tested the apartment for mold prior to moving in. I was still quite sick. Somehow, I thought that magically getting out of the moldy house would make me well. Wrong. I remember lying in bed in the apartment, my husband working all day and taking care of me when he returned home. Feeling extremely discouraged, depressed, and hopeless, I felt like this was going to be my life. I could not pray.

We decided we had to build a new house. Thankfully, we were able to sell the house from hell and had enough money for a down payment. However, looking for homes in the area close to Brady's office (in Scottsdale) that we could afford was not possible. Most were older, and a few that we had tested for mold did, in fact, have mold. Approximately 50 percent of homes in the U.S. have mold. Not all homes have toxic mold, and many people do not react to toxic mold; my husband did not have any reaction to the toxic mold in our moldy house (Brady was taking Lupron during that time after his prostate surgery to keep his PSA decreased), but I sure did.

Consequently, we decided to build in Northwest Phoenix in a small new home division that was only about five minutes from where our son and his family lived. During the year, the new house was being built, Brady drove across town to check on the building process. Brady coordinated and bought furniture online when he could. We bought a couple of larger items at a local furniture store. We moved into our new home in February 2019.

I was researching health problems like mine (using my phone while still lying in bed) and read many people's experiences with mold and Lyme via the social networks. I was shocked at the thousands of people posting on these sites, how incredibly sick many were, and how many could not afford to leave a home or apartment with toxic mold. Many had tried to sue landlords after becoming sick with toxic mold, to no avail. Most of those posting did not have financial resources, and many were single parents with children. My heart ached for these people. My husband has been my caretaker, my best friend, and my soulmate. I am very thankful for him and his continued care for me—after his rare, aggressive cancer; sixteen-hour surgery; a death experience; and prostate cancer. He was in *much* better physical and mental health than I was.

New Home

It felt so good to be in a clean, *safe* environment—our new home. Our son and granddaughter came to the apartment to help us move to the new house. Brady and I felt like we had turned a corner; my health would improve. We bought an Austin air filter, which runs constantly based on the advice of Dr. Gray, who understood my illness. Now I was sure to get well. Behind our new home is Pyramid Peak, desert, and mountains. The view is a blessing every day.

However, I was not getting well as fast as I thought I should be. I was sure part of it was the trauma of losing everything we owned (we did keep some files, our wedding pictures, albums of my children, and other keepsakes in storage). My life was so different, my career gone. And the full-body pain returned. As I was lying in our new bed and started my prayer vigil again, I was at the end of my ability to continue—again.

My son and daughter-in-law told me about a pediatric neurologist in the Phoenix area. This neurologist was open to herbal as well as traditional medical treatments, so we made an appointment. She was very thorough in her testing and ordered a PET scan of my brain. Other physicians had not ordered a PET brain scan, though I had a CT scan of my brain, which was negative. Similar to the CT scan, the PET scan report of my brain indicated, "There is no evidence to suggest frontotemporal dementia, Alzheimer's disease, Lewy body dementia, or multi-infarct dementia. Impression: Negative scan of the brain."[20] This was good news but did not explain my symptoms.

When we were in the apartment, I bought Annie Hopper's DVDs, *Dynamic Neural Retraining System*, and started doing the exercises in the workbook that came with the purchase. Her system is based on her own experience with toxic mold and grounded in the neuroplasticity of our brains.[21] Interestingly, William James, in his work *Principle of Psychology*, written in 1890, first proposed the idea of the brain's ability to change.[22] Subsequently, contemporary authors have brought attention back to neuroplasticity, an incredible principle, which informed Annie Hopper.

While in our new home, and still in pain, I started daily work with Annie Hopper's workbook. I spent at least a half hour each day doing the exercises she recommended. I was absolutely amazed at the childhood memories that came back to me, memories that never would have come back without her exercises. They were great, won-

---

[20] This was my SimonMed PET Brain Scan Report as given on April 26, 2019.
[21] You can learn more on Annie Hopper's website, *DNRS: Dynamic Neural Retraining System* (retrainingthebrain.com).
[22] William James, *The Principles of Psychology* (New York: Henry Holt and Company, 1890).

derful memories—and I have never been able to remember much from my childhood! Her training sessions have helped many people. I was giddy as I could get while still being so sick, telling my husband about our neighborhood (we were born in the same town and knew each other as children). We knew everyone around us. It truly was a wonderful experience, but I was still in a great deal of bodily and head pain and, most days, could not get out of bed.

I started having heart palpitations. To rule out any cardiology problems, I had a complete workup with a cardiologist. Everything was normal. For me, as always, all test results were "normal," according to medically trained providers. One morning, I tried to get out of bed, and my legs would not hold me up. Luckily, I landed on our bed. My husband took me to the emergency room at a nearby hospital. The physician checked the usual and attributed my symptoms to stress; no labs indicated anything wrong—they were all normal. What a surprise. Pray more.

Our daughter-in-law once told me of a medical intuitive who had helped one of her friends. I was ready. Having never done anything like this before, I called a medical intuitive who lived on the East Coast and made a phone appointment. She had me complete some paperwork and relay some information.

Despite having been a trained social scientist, I was nervous about the appointment with Elizabeth. Then we began the phone appointment. I was completely amazed at what she knew about me, and when she told me that my small intestine was not digesting the food that I was eating, my disbelief turned to belief. In my years of phone research while sick in bed, I was acutely aware of "leaky gut." I knew she saw something in me that resonated with a great deal of what I had read. This medical intuitive had the skill to "see" what was going on inside. She was a gift.

I had been doing a great deal of research on my phone while lying in bed. A book that was especially helpful to me is *Toxic* by Neil Nathan, MD. Dr. Nathan provides a summary of the two leading pioneers in toxic mold illness[23], one of whom is Dr. Michael Gray, whom I was fortunate to see! Who knew?

Dr. Nathan's book provides a wealth of information about rebooting various body systems. TGF-β 1 is only one of the many lab tests that can help inform a provider about toxic mold, Lyme, and other similar illnesses. Most, if not all, general primary care physicians know nothing about these tests or illnesses, nor do most physician specialists. Interestingly, when Brady and I met with Dr. Gray, I told him that I was having electric shocks when I touched many items—even the washer, dryer, and dishwasher. Dr. Gray noted, as did Dr. Nathan, that electric shock sensations are common with mold toxicity. I knew Dr. Gray was the first physician to understand my illness; Brady and I were very thankful.

I had many of the symptoms described by Dr. Gray and listed in Dr. Nathan's book: muscle weakness, tingling in my left leg and both feet, dizziness, anxiety, depression, severe fatigue, severe headaches, and more. Dr. Nathan indicated, "Medical arrogance, alas, is such that if a patient describes something a physician has not studied, those symptoms are in the patient's head until proven otherwise."

That was it. Since I had been researching so much, I knew there was an excellent physician who had worked with Dr. Gray and was also a homeopathic/holistic physician: Mary Ackerley, MD, MD(H),[24] who specializes in toxic mold and Lyme disease. She was in Tucson, closer than Dr. Gray's clinic. I called and made an appointment; my husband and I drove to Tucson to see her. We spent quite a bit of time talking about everything that I had been through, and her last words to me were, "I think you have Lyme." I always suspected that I had Lyme disease and had several tests for it.

---

[23] Neil Nathan, *Toxic: Heal Your Body from Mold Toxicity, Lyme Disease, Multiple Chemical Sensitivities, and Chronic Environmental Illness* (Las Vegas: Victory Belt Publishing, Inc., 2018).

[24] Learn more from Dr. Ackerley's website, *My Passion 4 Health* (https://mypassion4health.com).

Lyme Disease

At our first appointment with Dr. Ackerley in 2019, we discussed my history, then she recommended lab tests, which I diligently completed. After reviewing my labs, at our next video appointment (COVID had started), she recommended quite a few supplements that I bought and took according to her protocol. One of the first questions she had asked me when my husband and I made our first visit to her was "Where did you grow up?"

"In the Midwest, the shores of Lake Michigan," was my answer. She nodded.

Within a couple of weeks of taking her protocol, I felt like a new person! Amazing! I had energy, the chronic fatigue seemed to be gone, and I felt like my old self! My husband and I took a long walk, something I had not done in over four years. I was ecstatic! However, after approximately three weeks, the energy faded, my fatigue returned, the pain returned—it all came back.

At our next appointment, Dr. Ackerley sent me an order for an IGeneX Lyme test in March 2020. It returned positive for Lyme. As I mentioned previously, I had a CDC test for Lyme, which was negative. So why was I now positive for Lyme? The CDC has recommended a two-step procedure for diagnosing Lyme: the ELISA and Western blot tests. According to CDC, "If this first step is negative, no further testing is recommended. If the first step is positive or indeterminate (sometimes called 'equivocal'), the second step should be performed."[25]

The CDC indicates five of ten bands for surveillance; however, 56 percent of patients with Lyme disease are negative via the CDC guidelines, and 52 percent of patients are negative for chronic Lyme disease tested by the ELISA guidelines but positive for the Western blot test. The percentage of people (52 percent) who test negative for

---

[25] Centers for Disease Control and Prevention, "Lyme Disease: Diagnosis and Testing" (https://www.cdc.gov/lyme/diagnosistesting/index.html).

chronic Lyme disease is astonishingly high. These findings suggest that the CDC guidelines are missing severely ill people.[26]

As IGeneX indicates, "There are multiple species and strains of *Lyme borreliae* (Lb). Therefore, tests must be targeted to these multiple species and strains to be able to detect them. If a patient is infected with a species or strain of *Lyme borreliae* that the CDC test cannot detect, they will get a false-negative test result and thus risk missing their diagnosis."[27] Additionally, according to IGeneX, the sensitivity and specificity of the CDC diagnostic guidelines are questionable. More species of *borreliae* are detected with IGeneX; thus, the better chance of an accurate diagnosis.

The results of my IGeneX Lyme ImmunoBlot IgG indicated there were six bands that were positive (23, 31, 34, 39, 41, 93). However, a positive CDC result for the ImmunoBlot IgG indicates that five or more of the following bands need to be positive: 18, 23, 28, 30, 39, 41, 45, 58, 66, and 93.[28]

Lyme disease is highly prevalent in the Northeast and Midwest U.S. At the time of this writing, I have lived in Arizona twenty-two years. So how did I acquire Lyme? I grew up on the southwestern coast of Michigan, a small, beautiful town on the shores of Lake Michigan. In addition to being at the beach a great deal in the summers, my parents took my sister and me when I was young to Deer Forest. Deer Forest was a place where we bought deer food and walked among the deer in a large, fenced area. At that time, no one was familiar with a tick bite, what it looked like or what the ramifications of it were. I'm sure my parents or even I noticed the classic bite; we would have watched it to make sure it went away—we likely attributed it to "bites from the beach." A reasonable conclusion at that time.

---

[26] Learn more about Lyme disease diagnosing on the patient-powered nonprofit website *LymeDisease.org* (https://www.lymedisease.org/lyme-basics/lyme-disease/diagnosis).

[27] "The Best Test for Lyme Disease," *IGeneX* (https://igenex.com/tick-talk/the-best-test-for-lyme-disease).

[28] March 11, 2020, IGeneX test results and interpretation.

Lyme disease is generally transmitted to humans and animals via tick bite, which is caused by the spirochaete Borrelia burgdorferi. A medical provider will generally tell a person who has been diagnosed with Lyme disease via the CDC guidelines that the prescribed treatment is antibiotics. For someone who knows what the tick bite looks like and is aware enough to get to a physician quickly, antibiotics may be a quick answer for treatment. However, peer-reviewed academic publications discuss the complexities of the disease and the challenges it presents, especially the problems with long-term antibiotic treatment.[29]

The positive results on my IGeneX test and having hung out at Deer Forest as a child all made sense. I have had anxiety most of my life, as well as "gut" problems and depression. The trauma of my husband's cancers, his death experience, losing all our belongings due to bad remediation of the house from hell, and the toxic mold itself likely blew up my system.

Ross Douthat in his Lyme memoir, *Deep Places*, writes,

> The incentive structures forged by the CDC were a fascinating case study in how bureaucracy shapes science as much as the other way around… The narrow diagnostic criteria became the benchmark not just for doctors treating patients but for researchers when they applied for public grants, so that Lyme research increasingly focused on the most certain diagnoses and left all ambiguous cases and potential false negatives alone. This approach ratified the establishment's confidence in their own rules of evidence. Likewise, after 1991, insurance companies began

---

[29] M. C. Van Hout, "The controversies, challenges and complexities of Lyme Disease: A narrative review," *Journal of Pharmacy and Pharmaceutical Sciences*, 21(305–515) (2018) (https://doi.org/10.18433/jpps30254).

to deny payment for Lyme cases that didn't meet the CDC criteria.[30]

Today, only with Medicare can some Lyme sufferers have a prayer of being covered by insurance (for the correct lab tests). The cost of holistic providers is prohibitive for most people; however, to get help from their suffering, they need a provider who looks outside the medical establishment to find answers; and most, if not all, are not covered by health insurance due to current guidelines.

Starting to Heal

After my three weeks of feeling great energy and after my Lyme diagnosis, Dr. Ackerley prescribed Japanese knotweed, which is inexpensive, along with many other supplements. Japanese knotweed is an herb and is well known to kill Lyme. In a *Frontiers in Medicine* 2020 study, twelve botanical medicines for Lyme disease were tested; Japanese knotweed was one. (See Notes)

I was thrilled to start an herbal medicine. Since I was very sick, it took me over a year to reach the prescribed dose of sixty drops of Japanese knotweed, at the rate of two times per day. When I started the drops, I could only take one to two drops once a day—in water. The herb hurt my stomach so badly it took me that long and one drop at a time to get to sixty drops twice a day, which I have now done for the last two years. I needed individualized care (as do most people with chronic Lyme, toxicity, and mystery illnesses) and monitoring from someone who knows about the devastating effects of toxic mold, chronic Lyme disease, environmental toxins, and mystery illnesses.

For the first time in years, in September 2021, I flew by myself to Portland, Oregon, to visit my daughter and her two children (my grandchildren) while my daughter's husband was out of town. I called myself a Lyft, got to her house, and stayed five days. My daugh-

---

[30] Ross Douthat, *The Deep Places: A Memoir of Illness and Recovery* (New York: Convergent Books, Random House, 2021).

ter, my grandchildren, and I hauled out in the rain to a pumpkin farm/patch where I pulled a heavy wagon with heavier pumpkins! All the while freezing. But I did it! Did I have normal energy when I returned home? No. I had to recover for about a week but was still able to do household chores. This would have been totally impossible the previous year.

For Christmas 2021, we went back to Portland to be with my daughter, our son-in-law, and grandchildren. We stayed a week and had a glorious time with them. Though I had energy and motivation to go to Portland to see my daughter and grandchildren, I was not yet out of the woods physically.

During the time I was seeing dozens and dozens of physicians, we spent thousands of dollars trying to find out what was wrong with me, and I had tons of needless medical procedures that cost a great deal of money and were ultimately not needed. During this time, I saw a physician who sold a device (for a thousand dollars) that he said would help the vagus nerve and lead to healing. He was certainly right about the healing power of the vagus nerve, but the device gave me migraines. He did not conduct labs (not sure that would have helped, since all were "normal" according to the medical establishment). However, this physician was informative and knew about severe inflammation (no health insurance accepted—all cash; what else is new?).

For over two years, I have had severe upper-abdominal pain, which was only present when I sat or lay down. I had a CT scan of my abdomen; everything was normal—of course. I now do vagal nerve exercises, based on the book *Accessing the Healing Power of the Vagus Nerve* by Stanley Rosenberg, who is a craniosacral therapist who has been practicing for over thirty years.[31] The exercises address anxiety, panic attacks, posttraumatic stress disorder, depression, the autonomic nervous system, bipolar disorder, and attention-deficit/

---

[31] Stanley Rosenberg, *Accessing the Healing Power of the Vagus Nerve: Self-Help Exercises for Anxiety, Depression, Trauma, and Autism* (Berkely, CA: North Atlantic Books, 2017).

hyperactivity disorder. The exercises are simple eye movements and neurofascial release.

According to *Live Science*, "The vagus nerve gets its name from the Latin word for wandering, which is appropriate, as the vagus nerve is the largest and most widely branching cranial nerve...and is the 10th of 12 cranial nerves that extend directly from the brain."[32] It is the largest nerve and carries information between the organs and the brain. The vagus nerve exercises helped me, though I still had a severe lack of energy. Even after very short walks, I am exhausted for several days until I build up some strength for another walk.

I'm sure that I have myalgic encephalomyelitis/chronic fatigue syndrome (ME/CFS), which affects millions of people. According to Dr. Ron Davis, "Too often, this disease is categorized as imaginary. When individuals with chronic fatigue syndrome seek help from a doctor, they may undergo a series of tests that check liver, kidney, and heart function, as well as blood and immune cell counts. All these different tests would normally guide the doctor toward one illness or another, but for chronic fatigue syndrome patients, the results all come back normal"[33]—like mine did. Dr. Davis, who is a partner in the Open Medicine Foundation's research, indicates that there were high levels of uranium in some patients' hair, *which was traced to contaminated well water.*[34] Yet most establishment medical providers believe that ME/CFS is in your mind.

All my labs from general medical providers all came back *normal.* It is extremely disheartening when a physician or nurse practitioner observes me with a "look" that communicates, *It must be in*

---

[32] Katherine Gould, "The vagus nerve: Your body's communication superhighway," *Live Science* (Sept. 16, 2022, https://www.livescience.com/vagus-nerve.html).

[33] Hanae Armitage, "Biomarker for chronic fatigue syndrome identified," *Stanford Medicine: News Center* (April 29, 2019, https://med.stanford.edu/news/all-news/2019/04/biomarker-for-chronic-fatigue-syndrome-identified.html?linkId=66719226).

[34] Cort Johnson, "Ron Davis's ME/CFS Moment: The 'Core Technology Disrupter' Gets a Win," *Health Rising: Finding Answers for ME/CFS and FM* (June 9, 2022, https://www.healthrising.org/blog/2022/06/09/ron-davis-mecfs-moment-core-technology-disrupter/).

your head, because all your labs are normal. These frontline providers are doing what they know. One of the many problems is that there is no adequate medical education about "mystery diseases/illnesses" that are not revealed by the normal lab tests.

Not all health problems show up on standard lab tests. I have had severe fatigue since 2015, when we moved into the moldy house, and have post-"exercise" malaise (I cannot *exercise* in the typical meaning of that word) and chronic fatigue, often associated with ME/CFS. Even after a brief walk, I am short of breath, and my head and stomach hurt a great deal. I had an endoscopy and colonoscopy to find out: both were clear. No problems. I then went to a cardiologist to rule out any heart issues. My dad passed away from a major heart attack, and heart attacks ran in his family, so a reasonable thing to do was rule out heart disease. The cardiologist I saw conducted many tests, such as the treadmill exercise, a nuclear medicine test, and an echocardiogram, and she tested me for POTS (postural tachycardia syndrome), common in mold/Lyme sufferers. All tests were normal; I did not have POTS, or any of the above-mentioned cardiac problems.

In 2021, I saw my medical provider, and she listened to my lungs and said they sounded fine, as had many other medical providers, but she suggested a pulmonologist anyway. It took three months to get an appointment with Dr. Timothy Bilcher of Pulmonary Associates in Phoenix. He was worth the wait. He is one of the kindest and most knowledgeable physicians I have ever seen. In March 2022, when he walked into my patient room (Brady was with me), he was extremely well prepared. He had done his research regarding past tests conducted on me and found the CT scan from 2015 that indicated a problem with the lower portion of my lungs. The physician who ordered the CT scan from 2015 did not say anything about my lungs and did not order any other test or recommendations for a remedy. I should have examined the CT report from 2015 and asked questions about it (I now always carefully examine each medical test report since then and ask the provider about the results if I don't understand them and/or if something was found in the report that was not discussed with me).

Without me saying anything about the toxic-mold house, Dr. Bilcher asked me, "Have you been exposed to mold?" *No other physician has even admitted that toxic mold can be very harmful,* and Dr. Bilcher, an expert pulmonologist, knew to ask me. When I told Dr. Bilcher that we had lived in the toxic-mold house for three years before finding out that there was a great deal of stachybotrys, aspergillus, and other toxic molds found behind the walls in the master bath—and about the botched remediation—he shook his head.

Dr. Bilcher ordered a high-intensity CT lung scan. The radiology report indicated no evidence of diffuse interstitial disease. However, a small 2.5mm ground-glass nodule in my left lower lobe was found. Also found was irregular pleural thickening in the left base adjacent to the posterior pleura with associated faint interstitial opacity within the lung of the posterior sulcus. This was slightly more prominent than it was on January 5, 2020, and might represent focal inflammatory change.

He prescribed two inhalers, which I started immediately. He also ordered a Southwest Allergy Panel, as well as a pulmonary function test. Interestingly, the results of the Southwest Allergy Panel indicated that I'm highly allergic to aspergillus (one of the toxic molds in the moldy house), ragweed, dust mites, elm trees, and juniper trees. Inhaling toxic mold in the house from hell had damaged my lung. Specifically, Dr. Bilcher indicated that the pain I experience in my upper stomach—the pain from the damage in my lower left lung—was due to the toxic-mold house.

When I first became sick in the toxic-mold house (2015), I knew my history with allergies and immediately went to an allergist in Phoenix who did the usual back-scratch test of foods. I was allergic to several foods, which I stopped eating immediately. However, the physician allergist did *not* order a Southwest Allergy Panel. I had weekly injections for food allergies only, but after approximately a year, I was getting worse; the shots were not helping my symptoms. Seven years, thousands of dollars, dozens and dozens of physicians, and I was not diagnosed with asthma and an allergy to aspergillus (and other environmental allergies) until March 2022.

I still see Dr. Vermani, the board-certified TMJ dentist, who is working to wean me off the good mouth guards. I also see Sari Lewis,[35] who is an excellent craniosacral therapist. She has been very helpful in calming my body and helping me to heal. I will continue to see Dr. Bilcher for regular checks on my asthma, lung inflammation, and nodule in my lungs. I am grateful that *at least* after seven years, Dr. Bilcher found my lung and allergy problems, that Dr. Ackerley ordered a Lyme test via IgeneX, and that Dr. Vermani and Dr. Cooper have helped me to chew again. My experience, as well as that of thousands of other people, demonstrates a *medical healthcare system that relies only on "normal" lab tests, which do not indicate severe illness for millions of people.*

I am still healing, but there has been progress, for which I am very thankful. I have a head tremor (diagnosed by two neurologists as essential tremor—and two other neurologists as cervical dystonia), which also quite coincidentally became very bad when we moved into the toxic-mold house. When I asked each neurologist what the tremor/dystonia was caused by, the answer was, "We don't know."

After years of supplements, lowered body inflammation, organic foods, no dairy, increased (vegan) protein, rest, and very slow recovery, I tried Botox again in January of 2023, with a new board-certified neurologist in Phoenix, Dr. Rebecca Jones. My tremor was so bad, I had been taking 0.5 clonazepam three to four times a day, but I didn't care. Anything that would stop my constant headshaking (I have broken half our glassware) was worth another try. However, I still cannot take Botox for my tremor.

As I stated earlier in this chapter, I have had depression (probably due to lifelong chronic Lyme disease) and had been taking SSRIs (Lexapro) for quite a few years. In 2019, I changed to Pristiq (SNRI) after reading the following study. After a study of the association between antidepressants and movement disorders using the World Health Organization (WHO) Pharmacovigilance Database, the authors' conclusion is: "The association between nine subtypes of movement disorders (akathisia, *bruxism*, dystonia, myoclonus, par-

---

[35] Learn more on her website *Sari Hands PLC* (www.sarihands.com).

kinsonism, restless legs syndrome, tardive dyskinesia, tics, *tremor*) and antidepressants…described as able to induce movement disorders, and drugs used to treat movement disorders" was analyzed (italics mine). The authors found "a significant increase for antidepressants in general for all subtypes of movement disorders, with the highest association with *bruxism* (teeth grinding/TMJ/TMD) and the lowest with tics. When comparing each of the classes of antidepressants with the others, a significant association was observed for all subtypes of movement disorders except restless legs syndrome with serotonin reuptake inhibitors (SRIs) only."[36] I have slowly titrated off Pristiq and will try an herbal remedy.

There have not been enough sufficiently rigorous scientific studies between essential tremors and environmental pesticides, toxins, and other herbicides. A peer-reviewed article in *PubMed*, "Tremorgenic Syndromes in Livestock,"[37] points to an environmental link to tremors in livestock. Interestingly, this article postulates that tremorgenic syndromes in livestock are related to grass, specifically, white snakeroot and rayless goldenrod, which pose significant health threats to humans drinking cow milk. By the time an individual develops tremors (voice, hand, and head are the most common tremors), it may be too late for significant help.

I have tingling in my left leg and both feet, and, interestingly, my left ear and left side of my face will flush and become very hot when I wake up, and generally this also happens in the evening. I have vision loss in my left eye, but it has been better having been diagnosed with dry eyes and using preservative-free eye drops day and night. I have had vertigo, migraine headaches, weakness in my legs, general overall weakness, and extreme fatigue.

My vertigo has tapered off, thankfully. A visit to my physician assistant at my ENT's office when I had my first "hit" of vertigo (I

---

[36] A. Revet, et al., "Antidepressants and movement disorders: A postmarketing study of the world pharmacovigilance database," *BMC Psychiatry*, 16:20(1) (2020).

[37] S. S. Nicholson, "Tremorgenic syndromes in livestock," *The Veterinary Clinics of North America: Food Animal Practice,* 5(2), (2020), doi: 10.1016/s0749-0720(15)30977-4.

could not sit up, stand up, and was near vomiting) was productive. She had me lie on my right and left side; the left side was the worst (I now only sleep on my right side). On the left side, she performed the left Epley maneuver.[38] My vertigo is caused by benign paroxysmal positional vertigo (BPPV). The inner ear contains calcium crystals that sometimes become detached and go to the semicircular canal in the inner ear. This process sends incorrect "signals" to the brain, which causes vertigo. Doing the Epley maneuver has worked every time for me, though it may take a few times during the vertigo episode. Please check with an ENT to make sure this is the cause of your vertigo.

I am making slow progress, after thousands of dollars, undergoing *needless* and expensive medical procedures, consulting with physicians who did not know anything about toxic mold and chronic Lyme, diving down many rabbit holes, and taking *much* too long to be diagnosed with all that I have going on.

My suffering, physical, mental, and emotional, has led me to deeper faith and trust in God, the Divine. Neither Brady nor I believe God *causes* suffering; however, when suffering comes, as it likely will to most people, it can not only release our attachments to material "things" but loosen other attachments as well. For me, my attachments to fear—that Brady would die before me, and that I would never again be without some pain in some part(s) of my body—needed to be released. I am learning to trust God, or the Divine, on a daily and hourly basis. I am finding joy in watching the hummingbirds in our backyard, joy in watching the clouds, immense joy in Brady's strength and energy and love for me, my children, and grandchildren. There is joy in seeing the beautiful bougainvillea in our backyard, joy in my ability to walk (not much, though) without collapsing, joy in being able to socialize occasionally with our good friends, joy in writing to you about our story.

---

[38] Learn more from "What is the home Epley maneuver?" on the *Johns Hopkins Medicine* website (https://www.hopkinsmedicine.org/health/treatment-tests-and-therapies/home-epley-maneuver, accessed March 26, 2022).

Our teacher and pastor, Dave Brisbin, says it best in his book *Daring to Think Again*:

> As creatures of a broken heart, the truth that the Way to healing is actually down and not up, a letting go rather than an acquisition, an admission of vulnerability, a lowering of imagined position, is just too frightening to accept if we believe we have any power left to defend. But when the first wall comes down, and instead of the hordes of the enemy we have feared so long, we are greeted with a limitless view of ocean, we are at first still terrified with the dawning of our own seeming insignificance. But if we will stay on that shore, not run back to the fortification of womb and well, our eyes will slowly adjust to the brilliance of the light, and we will stand blinking and squinting and eventually smiling with all the other vulnerable ones who have come to know they are finally on their way home.[39]

Richard Rohr echoes the same concept: "But the only people who can experience 'Real Presence' are those who are vulnerable and don't have any ego boundaries to defend."[40]

Yet another author who has been very sick says it this way: "To those living in a culture that loves ascending, rising up, staying positive, practicing optimism, and revering strength, *down* can be a dirty word. But from the point of view of the soul, down is *holy ground*."[41]

---

[39] David Brisbin, *Daring to Think Again: Restoring Jesus' Original Challenge to the Faith We Think We Know* (independently published, 2019), p. 102.

[40] Richard Rohr, *Beginner's Mind* (Albuquerque, New Mexico: Center for Action and Contemplation, 2002).

[41] Lissa Rankin, *Sacred Medicine: A Doctor's Quest to Unravel the Mysteries of Healing* (Boulder, Colorado: Sounds True, 2022), p. 2, Kindle.

EPILOGUE

Beth

Brady and I have experienced two profound paradoxes in our illness journeys. The first is encountering divine presence through suffering, pain, and, in Brady's journey, death. As noted previously, our culture values strength, upward mobility, material possessions, money, and much more. However, for us, encountering divine presence was the opposite: a deep internal dive down. None of us want to do this. I thought that since I had some profound spiritual experiences in my life, I was on the "right path." Through my suffering and pain, I certainly learned that I needed to be humbled and vulnerable, and I had to let go of my attachments.

Brady

Beth and I have experienced some dramatic changes in our lives; both in our communal life together and in our individual lives. In our relationship, we have found ourselves much, much less concerned with some of life's trivial aspects as compared to the time before our illnesses. The absence for needless worry and unfounded angst has left so much room for joy, peace, and some profound experiences of presence with one another. For me, the change is a process. What I learned was a beginning for me as to how to follow a way of living which, I believe, is helping those around me. I experience myself as coming out of a fog of attachments and distractions of a material nature; I am more aware of divine presence, not just of every person but of everything.

Beth

The second paradox that we encountered is the excellence and brokenness of the traditional medical healthcare establishment. The juxtaposition of Brady's illness journey and my illness journey vividly conveys the stark reality of two different medical worlds. Without Brady's renown oncologists and surgeons at MD Anderson Cancer Center in Houston, he would certainly not be alive today. The phenomenal expertise of these specialists is nothing short of miraculous. Many people from around the world come to MD Anderson Cancer Center in Houston for the best cancer care in the world. There are other Centers for Excellence for cancer care with experts that can be found at the National Cancer Institute, a part of the National Institutes of Health.[42]

Medical science has saved countless lives, and, for example, made it possible for people without limbs to have an artificial leg or arm. These advances are, without question, incredible. Medical science labs are full of exciting new treatments for many diseases. In many respects, medical "silos" like Centers for Excellence in Cancer and cancer research are necessary for advancing disease cures.

However, *at the same time*, medical silos have hampered help for other illnesses and diseases. During the last seven years while battling my illness with toxic mold, Lyme disease, chronic fatigue, and enduring pain, I saw many physicians: primary care providers, neurologists, cardiologists, ENT physicians, physiatrists, dentists, and more. Each had expertise in a specific area of specialization. but none could determine the cause of my intense pain and suffering. The same is true for millions of other people. All medical establishment lab tests inform the medical conclusions from each physician's/provider's perspective. This is what each provider has been trained to look for and do.

Most humans are the same in terms of internal organs, eyes, arms, legs, brain, etc. However, *we differ genetically, in terms of individual sensitivities, extent of environmental and chemical exposures,*

---

[42] You can find NHI-designated Cancer Centers via the National Cancer Institute website (https://www.cancer.gov/research/infrastructure/cancer-centers/find).

tainted water supply, diet, and more. Regular lab tests are "normal" (i.e., do not provide insight or direction for an illness) for me and millions of people suffering with chronic illnesses. In addition to toxic mold and Lyme disease, another area of research that has been missing from medical school education is environmental toxins in our air, water, food, plastics, and in our clothing. In our polluted nation and world, how can this possibly be overlooked?

There is no evidence of cancer in Brady's family history: his parents, his grandparents on both sides—no one. Generally, genetics are a key indicator for cancer. We will never know what caused a five-pound (normally lethal) leiomyosarcoma to grow from Brady's right ureter. However, we speculate that it is from the environment. The appalling number of environmental toxins that we ingest, breathe, and wear on a constant basis cannot be ruled out for causing his massive tumor, sixteen-hour surgery, suffering, death experience, and prostate cancer.

The current state of the American medical establishment is falling short for thousands of people (like me), which is seriously and negatively affecting our health and society. Illnesses cannot be divorced from the environment in which we live. The American Academy of Environmental Medicine is one organization that is addressing the health consequences of our toxic environment and is very informative. Interestingly, the history of environmental medicine is traced to Theron G. Randolph, MD, who became interested after he smelled stench on his family's cattle farm that came from the Dow chemical company in Midland, Michigan.

The National Institute of Environmental Health Sciences (NIEHS) provides information on a wide variety of toxic environmental agents. However, in searching the NIEHS website for funding and research grants, I found that the link led to the Department of Health and Human Services, which focuses on establishing medical research opportunities, not on environmental health and how toxins affect our health. There are funding and research grant opportunities through the National Center for Complementary and Alternative Health, though most of the funding opportunities do not relate to toxins in our homes, air, food, plastics, and clothing—our everyday encounters with toxic substances.

The general public and medical schools must become more informed regarding the negative health effects of environmental toxins. This can only be accomplished by appropriate medical education, funded research, and public awareness of toxins that we ingest, breathe, and wear daily. Our country and world are in dire need of Preventative Environmental Toxicity as a specialization for all physicians/providers and functional/alternative providers.

As for our story: Brady is still working from home with a full schedule. He is an exceptional psychologist and is providing help to so many who need it. Brady just had (as of October 2022) his annual check with the phenomenal oncologists at MD Anderson Cancer Center in Houston. His PSA has increased from .3 to .4. However, a more recent PSA check indicated that .4 is stable, i.e., no increase, which is good. I am thankful he is alive, that he is helping others, is a wonderful dad, grandpa, husband, and my best friend and soulmate. He continues to be in great spirits, plays golf, and loves his work and his family. I am healing with the help of functional/alternative, dental, and medical providers and writing this book to, hopefully, help others, trusting in God, the divine presence, and being patient (patience has never been my major strength!).

Brady and I returned from a two-week trip to London, England, in July 2022 (which we had been planning for a year and a half prior to our trip). I was amazed at how well I did; Brady did great and always has much more energy than me. The trip was planned a year prior, and though COVID is still around, Brady and I got a second booster before we left for London. I had to sit down and rest periodically as we took in the sights, and I took my supplements and medications to help me make it. (I saw two very special friends from when Mom, Dad, my sister, and I lived in London—quite a few years ago). But I did it. I am very thankful and grateful for the progress that I've made with the help of God (the divine presence) and my providers.

Brady and I tested positive for COVID after returning to Phoenix, and we both took an antiviral, Paxlovid. Brady is doing great. However, COVID caused a flare in my pain, especially in my lower back, muscles, and temples, and greatly increased my fatigue. I made an appointment with Dr. Ackerley. She prescribed several supplements that are helping my fatigue. However, there are clinical trials and many scientific studies being conducted to identify a cure for long COVID.

Interestingly, Dr. Vermani, my *board-certified* TMJ dentist very recently indicated that I have a lingual restriction. This diagnosis was confirmed by a speech pathologist who is a certified orofacial myologist. What is a lingual restriction? It's a band of tissue between the tongue and the floor of the mouth that is too tight, effecting its ability to perform normal function properly. When there is a restriction, other muscles in the body will compensate for the lack of movement. This compensation can cause chronic pain throughout the body. I had a surgical frenectomy in June 2023 to sever the tissue, which is a minor surgery, with an oral surgeon. So, once again, in our extremely fragmented healthcare delivery system, I found out in May 2023 about yet another physical problem that contributes to pain (in addition, of course, to toxic mold, Lyme, etc.) and that is exacerbating my constant temple pain and tight "knots" in my upper back, shoulders, and who knows what else. Amazing.

Brady came away from his death experience with the profound sense that we are here to help one another. In other words: love one another; do unto others as you would have others do unto you; be kind to each other; recognize the soul in every being.

> Deep peace of the running wave to you.
> Deep peace of the flowing air to you.
> Deep peace of the quiet earth to you.
> Deep peace of the shining stars to you.
> Deep peace of the gentle night to you.
> Moon and stars pour their healing light on you.
> Deep peace of Christ to you.
>
> (A Gaelic Blessing)[43]

---

[43] John Rutter, sourced from Amaranth Publishing's webpage, where a choral MP3 of "A Gaelic Blessing" may be found (https://www.amaranthpublishing.com/GaelicBlessing.htm).

NOTES

1   My research in PubMed indicates a great deal of peer-reviewed medical journal
    articles regarding TGF-β. There are three types: TGF-β_1, TGF-β_2 and TGF-
    β_3. "The TGF-β proteins have been discovered in a variety of species, including
    invertebrates as well as vertebrates. TGF-β superfamily is fundamental in
    regulation of various biological processes, such as growth, development,
    tissue homeostasis and regulation of the immune system" (Y. C. Yang, et al.
    Transforming growth factor-beta1 in inflammatory airway disease: a key for
    understanding inflammation and remodeling, *Allergy, 67[10]*, 2012).

2   As noted on my IGeneX report and interpretation, "IGeneX, Inc. is licensed
    by the Centers for Medicare & Medicaid Services (CMS) and NYS to perform
    high complexity clinical laboratory testing." In 2019, the CDC updated its
    guidelines for Lyme disease diagnosis that included "using a sensitive enzyme
    immunoassay (EIA or immunofluorescence assay), followed by a western
    immunoblot assay for specimens yielding positive or equivocal results." The
    new CDC guidelines would not have diagnosed my Lyme disease. (You
    can access the updated CDC recommendation for Serologic Diagnosis of
    Lyme disease on their website: https://www.cdc.gov/mmwr/volumes/68/wr/
    mm6832a4.htm?s_cid=mm6832a4_w.)

3   In the April 26, 2022, edition of Lyme Disease Association, Inc., a remembrance
    of Dr. Nick Harris, the founder of IGeneX Labs, chronicled his courageous
    fight: "He was one of a few dissenters at the 1994 Dearborn Lyme disease
    testing meeting where government and Lyme denier researchers removed the
    31 and 34 bands from Lyme testing—bands which treating physicians knew
    were essential for diagnosis of Lyme disease, imposing a ludicrous testing
    standard still used today, an unbelievable 28 plus years later—an antiquated
    two tier testing regimen with 'banned' bands—a disaster for those trying to
    receive treatment." The removal of bands 31 and 34 has caused unbearable
    suffering for severely ill people who tested negative for Lyme; it is also why
    today Lyme disease sufferers cannot get insurance to cover their illness.

4   According to Feng et al., "The top two active herbs, *Cryptolepis sanguinolenta*
    and *Polygonum cuspidatum* [Japanese knotweed] showed strong activity
    against both growing *B. burgdorferi* (MIC = 0.03–0.06% and 0.25–0.5%,
    respectively) and non-growing stationary phase *B. burgdorferi*. In subculture
    studies, only 1% *Cryptolepis sanguinolenta* extract caused complete eradication,

while doxycycline and cefuroxime and other active herbs could not eradicate *B. burgdorferi* stationary phase cells as many spirochetes were visible after a 21-day subculture" (J. Feng, et al., "Evaluation of natural and botanical medicines for activity against growing and non-growing forms of B. burgdorferi," *Frontiers in Medicine*, 7(6), 2020; doi: 10.3389/fmed.2020.00006).

[5] A new study of depression and the serotonin theory casts significant doubt on the hypothesis that a serotonin abnormality in the brain is the primary reason for depression. According to Revet et al., "Our comprehensive review of the major strands of research on serotonin shows there is no convincing evidence that depression is associated with, or caused by, lower serotonin concentrations or activity." The authors conclude that "most studies found no evidence of reduced serotonin activity in people with depression compared to people without, and methods to reduce serotonin availability using tryptophan depletion do not consistently lower mood in volunteers." This is a remarkable study and finding. The serotonin theory of depression is still taught and accepted by most researchers and practitioners. Yet until this extremely detailed study, it might all be based on a false premise. Might depression be related not only to genetics but interaction with the environment based on each individual's physical condition, stress tolerance, exposure to air, food, clothing, and all environmental toxins, as well as life's difficulties? It seems the answer may be far more complex than previously thought. Antidepressants and movement disorders: A postmarketing study of the world pharmacovigilance database (*BMC Psychiatry, 16:20[1], 2020*).

RESOURCES

NOTE: *We are NOT functional/holistic providers OR medical physicians.* However, we both have been severely ill and have done a great deal of health research.

For anyone

- Please visit Brady's website at http://www.cbradywilson-phd.com.
- The International Agency for Research on Cancer (https://www.iarc.who.int/about-iarc-mission/) from the World Health Organization provides invaluable publications on many different kinds of chemicals we are exposed to and that are known carcinogens.
- For people who have cancer, you can self-refer to MD Anderson Cancer Center in Houston (please don't go to any of the satellite clinics); however, you will need to have a biopsy and send the results of the biopsy with your self-referral to MD Anderson Cancer Center. Visit https://www.mdanderson.org/. It is number one in the nation for cancer care.
- Over 50 percent of the homes in the U.S. have mold. Some people will be severely affected by it; some won't. Many people who are affected do not know their symptoms may be from toxic mold.
- Check your home for mold. We use Mycometrics.com; however, also check the ISEAI's website for their recommendations (https://iseai.org/finding-the-right-indoor-environmental-professional-to-assess-your-home/).

- Visit the ISEAI (International Society for Environmentally Acquired Illness) website for their own resource page (https://iseai.org/patient-resources/).
- Leave your vent on after showering. We leave ours on for at least an hour after we take showers.
- Get an air filter for your home; we leave ours on twenty-four seven (except when we clean it).
- We transfer all food that comes in plastic wraps or containers to glass containers.
- If you have a gas stove, be sure to always have the vent above the stove on during cooking. We turn off our gas (at the source) for the stove when we are not using it.
- Please buy cloth (not plastic) grocery bags to take to the store. You can buy cloth bags for your veggies and fruit. You will avoid using tons of plastic for groceries, saving your health and the planet.
- We take off our outdoor shoes every time we enter the house, so we are not tracking pollen and outdoor pollutants throughout the house. We have indoor shoes and outdoor shoes. This system does not prevent pollutants from entering from the outdoors, but it helps.
- If your car has a HEPA filter, be sure to get it changed regularly and make sure it is on when you are driving.
- Please check the Environmental Working Group (ewg.org) for healthy choices regarding food, water, farming, agriculture, personal care products, household and consumer products, energy, family health, toxic chemicals, and regional issues.
- Earthjustice (earthjustice.org), a nonprofit organization, has a team of one hundred eighty environmental lawyers focused on national and regional issues.
- Donna Eden has written *The Little Book of Energy Medicine* (Jeremy P. Tarcher/Penguin Books, 2012). Donna also has YouTube videos in which she demonstrates her energy medicine exercises (check out her channel *Donna Eden*

Energy Medicine on https://www.youtube.com/channel/UCn_yr5l2SQJdW6llBOI1I9Q).

- Dr. Lee Bartel has been conducting fascinating studies in sound vibration—music and its neurological, physiological, and biochemical effects on humans. He discusses his research on YouTube. You can see his TED talk on "Music Medicine: Sound at a Cellular Level" at https://www.youtube.com/watch?v=wDZgzsQh0Dw&ab_channel=TEDxTalks (accessed May 31, 2023).
- Visit the Center for Science in the Public Interest (https://www.cspinet.org).
- Visit the American Academy of Environmental Medicine (https://www.aaemonline.org).
- Visit the National Institutes of Environmental Health Sciences (https://www.niehs.nih.gov/).
- Kate Bowler and Jessica Richie wrote *The Lives We Actually Have: 100 Blessings for Imperfect Days*, (New York: Convergent, 2023).
- Richard Rohr wrote *Falling Upward: A Spirituality for the Two Halves of Life* (Jossey-Bass, A Wiley Imprint, 2011).
- David Brisbin wrote and independently published both *Daring to Think Again: Restoring Jesus' Original Challenge to the Faith We Think We Know* (2019) and *The Fifth Way: A Western Journey to the Hebrew Heart of Jesus* (2014).
- Please visit Mark Cuban's Cost Plus Pharmacy at https://costplusdrugs.com/. You will save hundreds of dollars on many medications. Beth gets one of her medications from this very helpful site.

For Lyme disease, toxic mold, ME/CFS, long COVID, and anyone who has a "mystery illness," i.e., no diagnosis by the medical establishment

- Find a Lyme-literate MD or functional medicine provider; visit the ISEAI website (iseai.org) for help.
- If you live in a wooded area, use a safe substance for tick avoidance. If you or one of your family members are bit-

ten, look for the classic round red ring and get to a Lyme-literate physician immediately.

- Some books to check out:
  - ¢ Nathan, Neil. MD. *Toxic: Heal Your Body from Mold Toxicity, Lyme Disease, Multiple Chemical Sensitivities and Chronic Environmental Illness.* Victory Belt Publishing Inc., 2018.
  - ¢ Rawls, Bill, MD. *Unlocking Lyme, Myths, Truths and Practical Solutions for Chronic Lyme Disease.* First Do No Harm Publishing, 2017.
  - ¢ Buhner, Stephen Harrod. *Healing Lyme.* Sheridan Books, 2015.
  - ¢ Weintraub, Pamela. *Cure Unknown: Inside the Lyme Epidemic.* St. Martin's Press, 2008.
  - ¢ Douthat, Ross. *The Deep Places: A Memoir of Illness and Discovery.* Convergent Books, an imprint of Random House, a division of Penguin Random House LLC., 2021.
  - ¢ Ramey, Sarah. *The Lady's Handbook for Her Mysterious Illness: A Memoir.* Anchor Books, a division of Penguin Random House LLC., 2020.
  - ¢ O'Rourke, Meghan. *The Invisible Kingdom: Reimaging Chronic Illness.* Riverhead Books, 2022.
  - ¢ Scher, Amy B. *This Is How I Save My Life Searching the World for a Cure: A Lyme Disease Memoir.* Gallery Books, 2021.
  - ¢ Rankin, Lissa, MD. *Sacred Medicine: A Doctor's Quest to Unravel the Mysteries of Healing.* Boulder, Colorado: Sounds True, 2022.
- Visit HealthRising (www.healthrising.org).

Visit the Bateman Horne Center at https://batemanhornecenter.org/education/me-cfs/.

Thanks to Dr. Bill Rawls, a Lyme survivor who documents seven agencies helping people to finance their Lyme costs: the Lyme Treatment Foundation, LivLyme Foundation, Lyme Light

Foundation, LymeAid 4 Kids, Ride Out Lyme, State Specific Lyme Grants, Sam's Spoons (for Pennsylvania residents), and Lyme Test Access Program. Visit Dr. Rawls's website (https://rawlsmd.com/health-articles/7-organizations-that-help-you-pay-for-lyme-treatment-testing).

Join a support group on social media or in your immediate area.

Toxins in clothing and textiles

- Visit the *Parachute* website to learn about Oeko-Tex, a textile certification standard (https://www.parachutehome.com/blog/oeko-tex-textile-certification).
- Visit the Organic Trade Association's website to learn about GOTS, or global organic textile standards (https://ota.com/advocacy/organic-standards/fiber-and-textiles/global-organic-textile-standard-gots).

Food

- Visit the Center for Food Safety website (https://www.centerforfoodsafety.org).
- Visit Sustainable Pulse (https://www.sustainablepulse.com).
- Dr. Michael Greger's *How Not to Die* (Flatiron Books, 2015) was recommended by Brady's sarcoma oncologist at MD Anderson Cancer Center in Houston.
- Alissa Segersten and Tom Malterre, MS, CN, wrote the *Whole Life Nutrition Cookbook: A Complete Nutritional and Cooking Guide for Healthy Living* (Grand Central Life & Style, Hachette Book Group, 2014).
- Also check out Melissa Hartwig's *The Whole 30: Fast & Easy* (Houghton Mifflin Harcourt, 2017).
- There are many more wonderful healthy cookbooks available; too numerous to list here. What has helped us is a diet based on organic fruits, vegetables, homemade soups, protein shakes (nondairy), ahi, salmon, no poultry, gluten-free crackers, and gluten-free bread (very little of both). We use

organic stevia for a sweetener and avoid all sodas and sugar products.

Climate

- Read David Wallace-Wells *The Uninhabitable Earth: Life After Warming* (Tim Duggan Books, an imprint of Random House, a division of Penguin Random House LLC., 2020).
- Visit the Bloomberg Green website for daily updates on climate activity worldwide (www.bloomberg.com/green).

ABOUT THE AUTHORS

C. Brady Wilson, PhD, is a licensed clinical psychologist practicing in Arizona for over forty years. His PhD is from Boston University, and his specialty in clinical psychology is working with trauma and anxiety reactions. Dr. Wilson was honored with the Karl F. Heiser Presidential Award by the American Psychological Association and has served as the president of the Arizona Psychological Association.

Beth H. Wilson received her PhD in organizational communication from Michigan State University, which had a strong social science focus. She was a co-winner of the prestigious W. Charles Redding Dissertation Award from the International Communication Association. She has many peer-reviewed academic journal articles and many peer-reviewed conference presentations (under the name Beth Hartman Ellis).

Printed in the USA
CPSIA information can be obtained
at www.ICGtesting.com
CBHW051235150824
13132CB00065B/1027

9 798888 518274